Landmarks of world literature

Honoré de Balzac

OLD GORIOT

Landmarks of world literature

General Editor: J. P. Stern

HONORÉ DE BALZAC

Old Goriot

DAVID BELLOS

Professor of French Studies
University of Manchester

CAMBRIDGE UNIVERSITY PRESS

Cambridge
New York   New Rochelle   Melbourne   Sydney

Published by the Press Syndicate of the University of Cambridge
The Pitt Building, Trumpington Street, Cambridge CB2 1RP
32 East 57th Street, New York, NY 10022, USA
10 Stamford Road, Oakleigh, Melbourne 3166, Australia

First published 1987

Printed in Great Britain at
the University Press, Cambridge

British Library cataloguing in publication data

Bellos, David
Honoré de Balzac: Old Goriot. –
(Landmarks of world literature).
1. Balzac, Honoré de. Le père Goriot
I. Title II. Series
843'.7   PQ2168

Library of Congress cataloguing in publication data

Bellos, David
Honoré de Balzac, Old Goriot.
(Landmarks of world literature)
Bibliography.
1. Balzac, Honoré de, 1799–1850. Père Goriot.
I. Title. II. Series.
PQ2168.B45   1987   843'.7   87–14687

ISBN 0 521 32799 7 hard covers
ISBN 0 521 31634 0 paperback

VN

The rule is that there are no good fathers;
it is not the men who are at fault but
the paternal bond which is rotten

Jean-Paul Sartre, *Words*

Or, le sentiment du Père Goriot implique la
maternité . . .   Balzac

Contents

Chronology

	Literature	Biography	History
1789			14 July: storming of the Bastille
1793			Execution of Louis XVI
1794			'The Terror': mass executions of real and suspected opponents of the Revolution
1799			Napoleon Bonaparte elected Consul
1805		20 May: Honoré Balzac born at Tours	Napoleon crowned Emperor of France
		Balzac sent as a boarder to the Collège des Oratoriens at Vendôme	
1812			French armies invade Russia
1813			French armies withdraw from Russia in disarray
1814	Walter Scott, *Waverley*	Balzac leaves Vendôme for a boarding school in Paris	Napoleon capitulates at Fontainebleau, Louis XVIII restored to the throne
1815	Jane Austen, *Emma*	At school in Tours, then Paris, where his family settle	Napoleon escapes from exile in Elba and leads reassembled army to defeat at Waterloo. Louis XVIII restored to the throne for a second time
1816		Apprenticed to the lawyer Guillonnet-Merville	

Year			
1819	Victor Hugo founds the *Conservateur littéraire* Walter Scott, *Ivanhoe*	Balzac's father, Bernard-François, retires. Honoré leaves the law practice and is allowed to stay in Paris 'to become a writer'. Writes *Cromwell*, a tragedy, published posthumously	
1820	Lamartine, *Méditations poétiques*	Begins *Falthurne* (unfinished)	
1821		Begins *Sténie* (unfinished)	
1822	Hugo, *Odes et poésies diverses*	Publishes novels written in collaboration under the pseudonyms of Lord R'Hoone and Horace de Saint-Aubin	Invention of Diorama
1823	Scott, *Quentin Durward*; Hugo, *Han d'Islande*; Lamartine, *Nouvelles méditations*	*La Dernière Fée*	Napoleon dies on Saint Helena
1824	Death of Byron at Missolonghi	*Annette et le criminel*	Death of Louis XVIII. Succeeded by his brother, Charles X First steam trains (Britain)
1825		Publishes Molière and La Fontaine in pocket editions; *Wann-Chlore*	
1826	Hugo, *Odes et ballades*	Buys a printing works	
1827		Sets up type-founding business	
1828		Businesses go into liquidation, leaving Balzac with heavy debts to his family	
1829		Death of Bernard-François Balzac; *Le Dernier Chouan*; *La Physiologie du mariage*. Balzac begins to visit the *salons* and to write for newspapers and reviews	

	Literature	Biography	History
1830	Stendhal, *Le Rouge et le Noir* (*Scarlet and Black*) Hugo, *Hernani*	*Scènes de la vie privée*, the first collective publication of stories. Many of them appear in the *Revue de Paris* and the *Revue des Deux Mondes*	Charles X overthrown in the July Revolution. Succeeded by Louis-Philippe d'Orléans
1831	Hugo, *Notre-Dame de Paris*	*La Peau de chagrin* favourably reviewed. Balzac now an established writer	Guizot's budget speech: 'Enrichissez-vous . . .'
1832	Deaths of Goethe and Walter Scott; George Sand, *Indiana*	Contacted by 'L'Etrangère', Mme Hanska. *Louis Lambert*, first version	Cholera epidemics in Paris and London
1833		Contract for 8-volume *Etudes de moeurs au XIXe siècle*; *Le Médecin de campagne*; *Eugénie Grandet*	
1834		*La Recherche de l'absolu*; *Le Père Goriot*	Signs of social unrest; Lyon silk workers strike
1835		*Séraphita*. Spends 3 weeks with Mme Hanska in Vienna *Le Lys dans la vallée*	
1836	*The Pickwick Papers*; Musset, *Confession d'un enfant du siècle*		
1837		*La Vieille Fille*; *Illusions perdues*, part 1; *César Birotteau*	First passenger steam train in France
1838	Dickens, *Oliver Twist*	*La Maison Nucingen*	
1839		Appointed president of the newly-formed Société des gens de lettres	Invention of photography by Daguerre

1840	Stendhal, *La Chartreuse de Parme*	*Vautrin* (a play); founds *La Revue parisienne*
1841		Signs contract for the full edition of *La Comédie humaine*; *Le Curé de village*
1842	Gogol, *Dead Souls*	*La Rabouilleuse*
1843		Completion of *Illusions perdues*; *La Muse du département*
1844		*Modeste Mignon*; *Les Paysans*; *Béatrix*
1845	Victor Hugo becomes *pair de France*	Travels to Germany, Holland, Belgium, Italy
1846	George Sand, *La Mare au diable*; Dostoevsky, *Poor Folk*	Italy, Germany again; *La Cousine Bette*
1847		*Le Cousin Pons*, completing volume 17 of the Furne edition. *La Dernière Incarnation de Vautrin*
1848		Travels to Mme Hanska's estate in the Ukraine	Louis-Philippe deposed in a revolution; Second Republic declared; Lamartine elected president
1849	Dickens, *David Copperfield*	In the Ukraine again, in poor health	Louis-Napoleon elected 'Prince-president'
1850		Marries Mme Hanska at Berdichev on 14 March. Returns to Paris on 20 May. Dies on 18 August	

Note on the text

Page numbers following quotations in French from *Le Père Goriot* refer to the Garnier-Flammarion paperback edition, GF 112, with an introduction by Pierre Citron, Paris, 1966. Translations are my own.

Quotations from all other works by Balzac are from *La Comédie humaine*, general editor Pierre-Georges Castex, Gallimard (Bibliothèque de la Pléiade), 12 volumes, 1976–81. This edition is designated by the abbreviation *Pl*, followed by volume number in roman figures and page numbers in arabic.

References to letters written and received by Balzac are to *Correspondance*, edited by Roger Pierrot, Garnier, 5 volumes, 1960–9, designated by the abbreviation *Corr* followed by volume and page numbers; and to *Lettres à Madame Hanska*, edited by Roger Pierrot, Aux Bibliophiles de l'Originale, 5 volumes, 1968–74, designated by the abbreviation *LH* followed by volume and page numbers.

Details of other works quoted, indicated in the text by the name of the author and, where appropriate, page number, will be found in the bibliography.

Introduction

Old Goriot is a complex work of art which seeks to represent the complexity of life. In this introductory study I will necessarily simplify Balzac's novel to some degree by explaining and discussing separately features which are woven into each other in the text itself. My aim is not to replicate the impact of *Old Goriot*, but to provide the modern reader with information which will help him or her to understand how complex Balzac's novel is. In Chapter 1, I deal principally with the processes which lead to the final shape and material of *Old Goriot*; Chapter 2 is concerned mainly with looking at four related aspects of what the novel achieves.

Balzac's novels have ceased to be easy texts for modern readers to understand and enjoy without effort. Because its action is in a social, historical, and geographical setting which was intended to be familiar to its original audience but is now dead and gone, *Old Goriot* presupposes a certain amount of knowledge which modern readers, by and large, do not have. Balzac's particular way of combining fact with fiction, descriptions of settings with character analyses, individual life with social environment, has had an enormous impact on the subsequent course of the European novel, and as a consequence on our own general expectations of what novels should be like, so that it is hard for us to perceive, let alone enjoy, the novelty and inventiveness of *Old Goriot*. Habits of language have also changed in the last hundred and fifty years almost as much as everyday habits, and these changes make it relatively difficult for a modern reader to respond appropriately to Balzac's stylistic verve and humour. As with all works of past ages, there is a danger that history in its various forms (social, literary, and

1

linguistic history) may have combined to transform *Old Goriot* from a living, complex work of art into a dusty and obscure museum piece. The aim of this book is not to brush aside the dust of history, but to provide the knowledge needed to read Balzac's novel in its own context. The effort of acquiring that knowledge is rewarded by the possibility of rediscovering a novel which integrates in a quite remarkable and moving way the fundamental conflicts of social life, and which still gives a masterful representation of the complexity of a world which, in the last analysis, is not very different from our own.

Old Goriot is a novel which weaves together three separate tales: the tale of Eugène de Rastignac, the young man starting out on life and learning how to make his way in Parisian society; the tale of Vautrin, a forty-year-old arch-criminal attempting to extend his power from its secret base in the underworld to control indirectly the life of a socially respectable young man; and the tale of the old man, Jean-Joachim Goriot, dying in poverty, unloved and unaided by his two daughters to whom he has given every ounce of his love, and every penny of the fortune he made in the flour trade. In 1819, when the action of *Old Goriot* commences, all three protagonists are lodgers at the boarding house of Madame Vauquer, a shabby and mysterious place located in one of the dark corners of the Latin Quarter, where nothing is quite what it seems, and certainly not what its proprietress, Madame Vauquer, claims it to be.

Eugène de Rastignac has set out with the best intentions and aims to make his way to the top through hard work, and to repay his family the sacrifices they have made to support him through his studies for a degree in law. But little by little, he lets his studies slip, as he is drawn at the start of his second year towards the glamour of the wealthy society of the *grande bourgeoisie* and the aristocracy which flaunts itself in the capital, and to which he has access by virtue of his nobility and a letter of introduction from his mother's aunt to a prominent society lady, Madame de Beauséant. Rastignac learns rather abruptly that 'high' society, like the 'low' society of the lodging house, is not what it seems. The wealthy and beautiful Anastasie de Restaud whom he meets at the first ball he attends turns out not only to be a commoner by birth, but the daughter of the retired flour-merchant who shares his lodgings in the Latin Quarter. Madame de Beauséant, noble and rich as she is, is also on the brink of despair and on the point of being abandoned by her lover, Ajuda-Pinto, for a younger and even wealthier bride. She advises Rastignac to seduce Goriot's other daughter, Delphine, the wife of a bourgeois banker, in order to establish his position in Parisian society. And that is what Rastignac does in the course of the novel.

Vautrin, whose real name is Jacques Collin, is lying low at the Vauquer lodging house after escaping from forced labour. He sees what it is Rastignac wants – wealth, position, prominence – and tells the young man in forceful terms that he will not achieve such ambitions honestly. All great fortunes, he claims, are the fruits of secret crimes neatly hidden. He offers the handsome student a deal: he will have the son of the millionaire Taillefer eliminated in a trumped-up duel, if Rastignac will seduce and marry the banker's daughter Victorine, currently disinherited by her father, and also lodging at the Vauquer house; in return, Rastignac would pay Vautrin a commission of twenty per cent on the million-franc dowry he would un-doubtedly extract from his father-in-law once the latter is bereft of a male heir. Rastignac hesitates; he has no feelings for the pallid Victorine, but the pact offers rapid access to a fortune which could only be got, if it could be got at all, through a lifetime of hypocrisy and petty crime. He hesitates for suf-ficiently long to fail to prevent the first stage of the plot taking place, and Victorine's brother is killed in a duel provoked on purpose by Vautrin's associate. But the arch-criminal is the most wanted man in Paris, and two further lodgers at the Vauquer house, Poiret and Michonneau, turn out to be informers and stool-pigeons; they trap the ex-convict, who is arrested and taken off by the police.

The story of how Goriot himself came to be a down-at-heel lodger in a shabby boarding-house whilst his two daughters lead lives of spendthrift luxury is revealed piece by piece through the discoveries Rastignac makes in his adventures and blunders in high society, through Vautrin's uncanny insight, and through the visits that Delphine and Anastasie make to the house. Once Vautrin has been removed from the scene and the Victorine plot put aside, the novel focuses firmly on the twin tales of the dying father and the ungrateful children. In a long monologue, Goriot goes over the story of his life as a parent and the issues it raises: had he done wrong by giving in to his daughters too easily in their childhood? Is he to blame for their present ingratitude? Or are they to blame for their own financial and emotional problems? Rastignac alone tends the dying man throughout his agony, but he also attends to Delphine and takes her to the great ball given by Madame de Beauséant, which represents to Delphine a satisfying revenge on her elder, aristocratically married sister. This close juxtaposition of splendour and squalor heightens the pathos of Goriot's death; the flashes of insight the old man has in his last moments into the nature of his daughters and of himself render his suffering properly tragic. The novel ends with Goriot's desolate funeral attended only by Rastignac and the empty carriages of two wealthy households, after which the young man of ambition, his education completed, walks back down in the city to proceed with his conquest of a mistress.

Chapter 1

The making of Old Goriot

The novel, the writer, and the reading public

It is hard to imagine a human society of any kind that does not have some way of telling stories. However, the particular form of story-telling that we now call the novel is of relatively recent date, and our present conception of it owes much to Balzac. Before him, of course, long stories written in prose and dealing with imaginary characters had entertained broad audiences for many centuries; but, with rare exceptions, prior to the nineteenth century, novels were considered by writers and readers alike as entertainment and not as part of serious literature, which tended to be restricted principally to drama and verse. The novel, before Balzac, was by no means a simple, homogeneous literary genre, but three main varieties can be identified: picaresque novels, such as Cervantes' *Don Quixote* or Fielding's *Tom Jones*, which recount the adventures of a usually male, and usually young, hero in more or less serious conflict with the society he finds himself excluded from; the novel of analysis, such as *La Princesse de Clèves* by Mme de La Fayette or, on a larger canvas, Rousseau's *La Nouvelle Héloïse*, dealing with the development of characters' inner feelings, most usually in connection with an amorous intrigue; and, in the eighteenth century, the parodic novel – Sterne's *Tristram Shandy* and Diderot's *Jacques le fataliste* are the best-known examples of this tradition – which creates sophisticated types of comedy by undermining and parodying the conventions of the picaresque and analytical novels. *Old Goriot* looks back to all three of these earlier kinds of novel in obvious ways: it tells the tale of a young man struggling to enter a society from which he is excluded, it offers insight into and analyses of the inner thoughts and feelings of Rastignac, Goriot and many other characters; and in several passages it draws on the tradition of self-critical humour. But *Old Goriot*, though it clearly draws on these various traditions, also introduces quite new features and organises them in a way that was not entirely without precedent, but had never been so strikingly combined before. Balzac's novel abandons the love intrigue as the central plot element of its analysis of feelings; it incorporates a properly tragic element in its principal narrative of the death of Goriot; and it brings an entirely new seriousness to the description of the physical setting in which its characters live. In these ways, *Old Goriot* marks a major development of the novel as a form, and contributes significantly to its emergence from the limbo of popular entertainment as the dominant form of serious cultural expression in the nineteenth century.

Of course Balzac did not achieve this transformation of the novel single-handedly, and throughout this study we will see how *Old Goriot* both resembles and differs from two other major novels written a few years earlier, Stendhal's *Le Rouge et le Noir* (1830) and Victor Hugo's *Notre-Dame de Paris* (1831). Nor did Balzac alter the status and form of the novel against the tide of other kinds of social and cultural change. On the contrary, many of the features which make *Old Goriot* such a significant landmark in European literature derive precisely from Balzac's ability to respond to the interests of a new audience.

The next section of this chapter, therefore, is concerned principally with the interaction of the writer and the reading public.

In September 1834, on doctor's orders, Balzac took a rest and went to stay in the country, at Saché, near Tours, the home of a close family friend, Monsieur de Margonne, the father of the novelist's ne'er-do-well, illegitimate half-brother Henri. Balzac had exhausted himself completing *The Search for the Absolute*, a novel whose hero, Balthazar Claës, sacrifices everything – including wife and family – to a single passion, the search for the mythical 'philosopher's stone' which would turn base metal to gold. This novel had had to be completed in a rush to fit into the publication of an eight-volume series of stories and novels, *Etudes de mœurs au XIXe siècle*, of which the first volumes had appeared in 1833 and included the masterly *Eugénie Grandet*. At Saché, though allegedly resting, Balzac thought out, or thought of writing, a short story under the title *Le Père Goriot* for the *Revue de Paris*.

The *Revue de Paris* had been founded in 1829, before the July Revolution of 1830, and aimed ostensibly to serve an aristocratic readership seeking relaxation. According to early publicity 'puffs' in other newspapers, its readers were recruited 'in the wealthy and relaxed portions of our society' and its pages offered 'a refuge where literature may retreat from the hurly-burly of our political camps' (Chollet, pp. 564–5). It was a very successful review, in a period when there was fierce competition amongst dozens of new periodicals for the favours of an increasingly large, and increasingly middle-class reading public. Some idea of the expansion of the potential field of literature can be drawn from a single statistic: the number of literate adults in France is estimated to have grown, in the half-century from 1780 and 1830, from seven to twelve million. It is almost certain that the success of the *Revue de Paris* rested not on the aristocratic readership it claimed to serve, but on a much broader, more diverse public, perhaps united by a snobbish desire to appear aristocratic, but brought into the ambit of the *Revue de Paris* essentially by the very high quality of the fiction it published, including texts by Stendhal, by E.T.A. Hoffmann (in Loève-Veimar's translation), by Mérimée and of course of Balzac, who was one of its principal suppliers of copy in the early 1830s. 'You will always be received with open arms at the *Revue de Paris* which will end up having a column erected in your honour on the place de l'Observatoire at the bottom of the Luxembourg gardens', wrote one of the editors to Balzac

(*Corr* I.535). So a short story for the *Revue* was essentially an easy and familiar assignment for Balzac to set himself in September 1834.

The real readership of the *Revue*, that is to say the original audience for which the story called *Goriot* was written, was probably as mixed and socially indeterminate as the audience for any successful work in the mass culture that was beginning to take shape in nineteenth-century France: it must have included students, who would read in lending libraries (there were no less than five hundred lending libraries in Paris alone in 1834), aristocratic and middle-class women with time on their hands, people in country houses on winter evenings, and – as we know from letters received by Balzac – readers scattered across Europe as far as the Ukraine, and across the world as far as Martinique. Nonetheless, the editors of the *Revue de Paris* had a notion of their 'target audience', a notion they used to impose stylistic and thematic constraints on their contributors. Some of the stories provided by Balzac (in 1830, 'Sarrasine', 'L'Elixir de longue vie', and 'Une Passion dans le désert'; in 1831, 'L'Auberge rouge' (see p. 37), and 'Les Proscrits'; in 1832, 'La Femme abandonnée' (see p. 38), 'La Grenadière', 'Madame Firmiani' and 'Voyage de Paris à Java'; in 1833, 'Ferragus'; and over the period several pieces that would be included in *La Femme de trente ans* and *The Wild Ass's Skin*, see p. 17) dealt with sexual matters, and the editors put pressure on the writer to be as discreet as possible: 'Our subscribers have not stopped being prudes despite the July Revolution, and in truth your style gives [the reader] erections' (*Corr* I.499) wrote Véron, the proprietor of the *Revue de Paris*, to Balzac. The review wanted, or reckoned its audience wanted, 'wit, style, interest, poetry', and did not want either explicit mention of sex or copious details. 'You will crush your rivals much more by the powerful interest of your stories than by the details you include', warned the editor Pichot (*Corr* II.225, 196).

These pressures, coming not directly from the reader but from what the publishers imagined the reader's taste to be, constituted both a challenge and an irritant to Balzac, whose own notion of what was important in his writing ran in a different direction. As early as 1830, when he was still hardly known, he had declared that 'the details alone' would be the worthwhile part of as-yet unwritten works for which the term *roman*, 'novel', had become inappropriate (preface to the *Scénes de la vie privée, Pl*I.1175, see p. 54). One of the ways in which Balzac met the challenge of editorial pressures and of an indeterminate readership was by appealing explicitly to a *fictional* audience, built into the construction of the tales being told in the *Revue de Paris*. The fictional audience of *Sarrasine*, for example, is a young woman of society, ignorant of the secret origin of the fortune of the Lanty family, at one of whose receptions she meets the narrator. He offers her knowledge of the secret in return for . . . well, the reader can surmise what s/he likes. By posing as an educator and seducer, the narrator of *Sarrasine* (and of other short tales for the *Revue de Paris*) creates his own ideal reader, out of a young man's fancy and a different grasp of the psychology of some real readers from the one held by the review's editors. The role thus inscribed into the text is there to be filled by any number of real readers – provided they are prepared to accept, provisionally, the position of a young woman seeking knowledge from a more experienced man.

The narrator of *Old Goriot* is clearly related to the seductive instructor of *Sarrasine*, but just as clearly he is a different person. He is less seductive, and more instructive; and as a teacher, he is aggressive and disapproving of his reader/pupil's tastes, tendencies, habits and expectations. In its final form, *Old Goriot* keeps some of the features of the short story it was originally intended to be, and in particular it begins in a way that suggests a sober and simple narrative construction. Four sentences set a scene: Madame Vauquer runs a boarding-house in Paris; the boarding-house is unusual, but respectable; young ladies have not lodged there for thirty years; but there was one there in 1819 (Balzac's arithmetic is notional – 1834 minus 1819 makes fifteen not thirty), when this story took place. Balzac uses a literary term, 'ce drame' (this drama), to refer to and characterise the not-yet-told story, and on the question of the appropriateness of that term (which the reader cannot yet judge) he hangs a bravura passage, often called in error the 'opening' of *Old Goriot*. In fact the novel 'opens' like a modern short story, with no explicit narrator; but as it turns back on itself (as a drama), a narrator emerges who has ceased to be the pliant seducer of the imaginary elegant lady-readers of the *Revue de Paris*, and who launches nothing less than an onslaught on the reader's competence.

Balzac loads the dice against the reader from the start. After the first four sentences any reader must assume that the last-mentioned 'poor young girl' will be the subject of the tale, at least initially. Since that is in fact a false assumption, the narrator's following attack is secretly justifiable. But why is Balzac so forcefully manipulative even behind the reader's back in this strange introduction to *Old Goriot*? The answers lie neither outside the text nor inside it, but in that important but elusive domain of interaction between reader and writer. Balzac is forceful here in order to signal the difference of this text from previous stories published in the same place; in order to call forth a different kind of reader and a different kind of reading. There's little point in making too fine distinctions between author, writer and narrator: Balzac *is* the narrator, struggling to break the chains that bind a mere supplier to his market, and to open up a new kind of contract with the public:

En quelque discrédit que soit tombé le mot drame par la manière abusive et tortionnaire dont il a été prodigué dans ces temps de douloureuse littérature, il est nécessaire de l'employer ici: non que cette histoire soit dramatique dans le vrai sens du mot; mais, l'oeuvre accomplie, peut-être aura-t-on versé quelques larmes *intra muros* et *extra*. Sera-t-elle comprise au-delà de Paris? le doute est permis. Les particularités de cette scène pleine d'observations et de couleurs locales ne peuvent être appréciées qu'entre les buttes de Montmartre et les hauteurs de Montrouge, dans cette illustre vallée de plâtras incessamment près de tomber et de ruisseaux noirs de boue; vallée remplie de

souffrances réelles, de joies souvent fausses, et si terriblement agitée
qu'il faut je ne sais quoi d'exorbitant pour y produire une sensation de
quelque durée. Cependant il s'y recontre çà et là des douleurs que
l'agglomération des vices et des vertus rend grandes et solennelles: à
leur aspect, les egoïsmes, les intérêts, s'arrêtent et s'apitoient; mais
l'impression qu'ils en reçoivent est comme un fruit savoureux promptement dévoré. Le char de la civilisation, semblable à celui de Jaggernat,
à peine retardé par un coeur moins facile à broyer que les autres et qui
enraie sa roue, l'a brisé bientôt et continue sa marche glorieuse. Ainsi
ferez-vous, vous qui tenez ce livre d'une main blanche, vous qui vous
enfoncez dans un moelleux fauteuil en vous disant: Peut-être ceci va-t-
il m'amuser. Après avoir lu les secrètes infortunes du père Goriot, vous
dînerez avec appétit en mettant votre insensibilité sur le compte de
l'auteur, en le taxant d'exagération, en l'accusant de poésie. Ah!
sachez-le: ce drame n'est ni une fiction, ni un roman. *All is true*, il est si
véritable que chacun peut en reconnaître les éléments chez soi, dans
son cœur peut-être.   (pp. 25–6)

(However much the term drama may have been discredited by the way
it has been lavished on everything, abused and twisted in these times of
painful literature, it must be used here: not that this story is dramatic in
the true sense of the word, but once the work has been read to the end
perhaps some tears will have been shed in Paris *intra muros* and *extra*.
Will it be understood outside of Paris? one may doubt it. The specific
details of this scene, full of observations and local colours, can only be
appreciated between the hills of Montmartre and the heights of
Montrouge, in this illustrious vale of plaster for ever on the point of
collapse and gutters black with mud; a valley filled with real suffering,
with joys that are often false, and so fearfully agitated that something
quite exorbitant is required to produce a sensation lasting any time at
all. Nonetheless, here and there, you can find suffering which the
compounding of vices and virtues renders great and solemn: before
them, people's egoism and self-interest halt and take pity; but the
impression made is like a juicy fruit, quickly swallowed. The chariot of
civilisation, like the chariot of Juggernaut, barely slowed down by a
heart less easy to crush than the others and catching on its wheel, soon
breaks it and proceeds on its glorious route. And that's what you'll do,
you who are holding this book in your fair hand, you who are settling
into a soft armchair and saying: Maybe this will entertain me. After
reading of the secret misfortunes of Old Goriot, you'll dine with a good
appetite and ascribe your insensitivity to the author, berating him for
exaggeration, accusing him of fantasy. But listen here: this drama is
neither a fiction nor a novel. *All is true*, it is so truthful that everyone
can recognise its elements in themselves, in their hearts, perhaps.)

The would-be elegant reader of the *Revue de Paris* (fair or 'white' skin, soft armchair) is told that she will behave like the spectacular chariot of the Indian idol Juggernaut as it processes, and will barely notice as a great and solemn passion is crushed beneath the wheels of 'civilisation'. That is no seduction, but a challenge to the reader to 'halt and take pity': s/he must read on in order to prove the narrator's prediction wrong, or else accept an equivalence that must have seemed intolerable between the material and intellectual softness of the wealthy classes and the cruel machine of modern civilisation. (We are a long way, here, from the connections Marx would make later on in the nineteenth century between the living conditions and ideology of the leisured classes, and the cruelty of the actual machinery of early capitalist society; but Balzac does sometimes allow the modern reader to discover with hindsight surprisingly progressive implications in his texts, even though his explicit political opinions were reactionary, monarchist and absolutist.) It seems to me that Balzac's attack on his reader is not a clever seductive ploy. The novelist had no reason to be certain that his readers would pick up the challenge in a playful way (and he was puzzled by the enormous popularity of the novel amongst Parisian readers: see *LH* I.310). He really does want to break the confidence of readers seeking only entertainment, and to lose them if they are not prepared to follow him into the adventure not of fiction, but of truth.

Balzac says in the passage quoted above that his tale will offer two kinds of truth. First, 'specific details' ('particularités'), which will only be appreciated in Paris, by readers who already know the city. This clearly is a seductive ploy, a minor challenge to read on and to learn those details, especially if one is not Parisian and wants to appear to be so (why else did the *Revue de Paris* sell copies in the provinces and abroad?). And it is a challenge immediately inscribed in the text: you have to know, or you have to guess, that 'Paris *intra muros*' refers to the central part of the city within the old boundary walls, and '*extra* [*muros*]' to the parts outside the boundary walls; that Mont-martre is a hill on the northern edge, Montrouge on the southern edge, and that the valley of the Seine, though it meanders, proceeds overall in an east–west direction through the city. 'Specific details' are there both to close off the text to an ignorant readership, and to open up Paris (but also much else) to readers wanting to learn.

Secondly, the narrator does more than to promise that his text will contain that kind of general and emotional truth that any reader can recognise by introspection: something like the truth of the heart, which is the traditional apanage of great works of literature. But as we saw at the start of this study, in Balzac's day (after Cervantes, Fielding, Richardson, Rousseau, Scott, Jane Austen . . .) novels were still regarded in France as essentially secondary, unserious works without the high pur-pose of stage tragedy. Therefore, in order to make his readers recognise *Old Goriot* as a work of high seriousness and to make them respect its emotional content, Balzac dissociates it as far as he can from a literary genre with an unserious reputation. The argument given here is much the same as what he said in a dozen other prefaces and introductions: call my works dramas, or histories, or what you will, but do not think of them as *romans*, in the sense of mere inventions or fantasies or idle fictions. The novel-reader picking up a new novel by Balzac to be entertained into an imaginary world is not the reader Balzac wanted for *Old Goriot*. He admits that his text is not dramatic 'in the true sense of the word', that is to say it is not actually a play; but he insists that it is not novelistic in the conventional sense either.

Balzac tries to make his reader see *Old Goriot* in terms of the values and content of stage drama by slipping in an allusion to Shakespeare, whose plays were regarded in the Romantic period in France as more true to life and more modern than the tragedies of Racine in the classical French tradition. His attempt fails for the English reader because *All is True*, given in English in the French text, is not the title of a play by

Shakespeare: but it was the title used in France at the time for an adaptation of *Henry VIII*. Ironically therefore one thing that is not 'true' in *Old Goriot* is 'All is true' . . .

It is partly because of slips of this kind that Peter Lock, in his study of *Old Goriot*, describes the author–narrator thus:

> Balzac, even in his modest moments, is always close to the stage; and for much of the time he bestrides his world like a Colossus, playing the parts of showman, propagandist, manipulator, prophet and sage.
>
> (Lock, p. 51)

This is an amusing and not inaccurate construction of the narrator's trades, but it is a list that seems also heavily loaded with a kind of middle-class disapproval. What we now know of the conditions originally envisaged for publication in the *Revue de Paris* explains in part why Balzac is an aggressive narrator; but it is curious that Lock omits the central, original and entirely reputable role of the narrator of *Old Goriot*, that of teacher. What the novelist claims to know in the passage studied, and in other places throughout *Old Goriot*, is the truth; and what he claims about his novel, which is not a novel, is that it will teach the truth that the reader already knows in her/himself. The narrative is the vehicle of the reader's education; the narrator gives the guarantee of its authenticity.

How Balzac wrote *Old Goriot*

There are eight extant versions of *Old Goriot*: all modern editions reproduce the last of the eight, corresponding to Balzac's final corrections around 1845, rather than the 'original' version of the novel, which would in any case be impossible to identify, as the inset table shows. In fact the novel went through many more than the eight listed versions, in the writing of the manuscript and no doubt in the correction of proofs for the *Revue de Paris*, which have not survived. Though these other hypothetical stages in the composition of *Old Goriot* cannot be laid out in tabular form, some parts of the story of the novel's writing can be reconstructed.

Table 1. *The texts of* Old Goriot

Version

I The 'Sina sheet' (*feuillet Sina*) consists of sheet 1 of the manuscript of *Old Goriot* used as an envelope for a letter to Balzac's lover, Mme Eve Hanska, posted in December 1834 care of 'Monsieur le baron Sina, Vienna, Austria'. It gives the earliest known state of the beginning of the manuscript, with an epigraph that was later abandoned: 'This is how the world honours misfortune: it kills it or rejects it; it cheapens or punishes it.'

II The manuscript, of 176 sheets in all, dated 26 January 1835 on an unnumbered covering sheet.

III The first printed version published by the *Revue de Paris* on 14 and 28 December 1834, 25 January and 11 February 1835. This version is divided into four parts: 'Une Pension bourgeoise'; 'L'Entrée dans le monde'; 'Trompe-la-mort'; 'Les Deux Filles'; part one contains two chapters ('Une Pension bourgeoise'; 'Les Deux Visites') as does part four ('Les Deux Filles'; 'La Mort du père').

IV First book publication, Werdet, March 1835, in seven chapters: 'Une Pension bourgeoise', 'Les Deux Visites', 'L'Entrée dans le monde', 'L'Entrée dans le monde (suite)', 'Trompe-la-mort', 'Les Deux Filles', 'La Mort du père'.

V Second book publication, Werdet, May 1835, with four section headings: 'Une Pension bourgeoise'; 'L'Entrée dans le monde'; 'Trompe-la-mort'; 'La mort du père'.

VI New edition, Charpentier, 1839, with corrected text; the preface and all internal divisions are suppressed.

VII 'The Furne', 1843. Balzac brought all his stories and novels together in a single publication entitled *The Human Comedy* and published in seventeen volumes from 1842–6 by a consortium of publishers: Furne, Dubochet, Hetzel and Paulin. *Old Goriot* appeared in volume IX, with the text further amended.

VIII 'Corrected Furne', or *FC*: the last emendations made by Balzac on his personal copy of the Furne edition, probably after 1845, and used as the basis for all modern editions.

What is almost certainly the first trace of Balzac's novel is an undated jotting in his notebook (later published under the invented title *Pensées, Sujets, Fragments*) which reads:

Sujet du Père Goriot. – Un brave homme – pension bourgeoise – 600fr. de rente – s'étant dépouillé pour ses filles qui toutes deux ont 50.000fr. de rente – mourant comme un chien.

(Subject of Old Goriot – A good man – middle-class lodging-house – 600 fr. income – having stripped himself bare for his daughters who both have 50,000 fr. income – dying like a dog.)

This was presumably the kernel from which Balzac expected a short story to grow fairly quickly, during his stay at Saché. Whilst there, he wrote in letters that he would have finished the tale by early October, but no trace remains of a short story version, if there ever was one. The subject grew into something that would require much more length; in early October Balzac wrote to his printer telling him to expect a text as long as *Eugénie Grandet*, and that the first thirty sheets, which were ready, would constitute about one-third of the total. In fact the first thirty sheets constitute something like one-fifth, not one-third, of the final manuscript. Balzac habitually underestimated the time he would take to finish his projects, and he habitually underestimated their final length. But with *Old Goriot* there was an unhabitual reason for the overshoot: something happened in the course of writing that was to have far-reaching consequences not just for *Old Goriot* but for all of Balzac's subsequent writing and for the European novel as a whole.

The manuscript II begins, as does the final version of the novel, with a long description of the Vauquer lodging-house and its inhabitants, who include a young law-student from Angoulême named Eugène de Massiac. Massiac is the character through whose observations and actions some of the links between the boarders and the world of fashionable society are explored. On sheet 17 he calls on Madame de Beauséant, a fictional character whose later life had already been invented in *La Femme abandonnée* of 1832 (see p. 8). A little later he meets

Anastasie de Restaud, who had already figured in a story entitled *Gobseck*, and is introduced to the marquis de Ronquerolles, one of the characters of *Ferragus*, published in 1833. Then comes, in a *salon* conversation, a list of the fashionable young men already invented in previous published stories and novels, including Eugène de Rastignac who had figured as a successful and cynical man-about-town in *The Wild Ass's Skin*, set in 1830. Finally, on sheet 43, Balzac crosses out Massiac's name and decides that his observer-hero in the story of old Goriot *is* Rastignac, but ten years younger than in his previous (and so far unique) appearance.

The invention of the 'reappearing characters' was then not quite the sudden flash of inspiration some critics (beginning with Balzac's sister, Laure Surville) have made it out to be, but a succession of logically-connected steps which the manuscript II clearly shows. It begins with the establishment of links between the fictional characters invented by Balzac as representatives of what was indeed a small world, that of high society: *grandes dames* such as Madame de Beauséant and successful dandies were almost by definition few in number in the real world, and Balzac's idea seems to have been, in the first instance, simply to reproduce that smallness in his fictional world. What does seem to be an inspiration is the decision on sheet 43 to make the observer of Goriot's tragedy into a character already possessing a future; and from this point on Balzac would seek in all his writing to link stories to each other by using at every opportunity characters whose lives had been or were to be told in part elsewhere. In the huge but manifestly incomplete *Human Comedy*, consisting of eighty-nine different novels and stories, Balzac created a cast list of well over two thousand named individuals, including about five hundred who appear in more than one text, and several dozen major figures whose lives are fragmented into stories spread through several texts. The invention of the device or the machine of the 'reappearing characters' took place in the actual writing of *Old Goriot*, and it is a major influence on, and a part of, the novel's form.

Table 2. *The reappearing characters of* Old Goriot

Cast	Principal reappearances
Marquise d'Aiglemont	*La Femme de trente ans, Le Lys dans la vallée, La Maison Nucingen*
Marquis d'Ajuda-Pinto	*Splendeurs et misères des courtisanes, Béatrix*
Vicomtesse de Beauséant	*La Femme abandonnée*
Vicomte de Beauséant	mentioned in *Etude de femme, La Femme abandonnée*
Horace Bianchon	*La Muse du département, La Messe de l'athée, Une Double Famille, La Peau de chagrin, Les Employés, Le Curé de village*
Lady Brandon	mentioned in *Le Lys dans la vallée, Mémoires de deux jeunes mariées*
Duchesse de Carigliano	*La Maison du Chat-qui-pelote*
Derville	*Gobseck, Un Début dans la vie*
Marquise d'Espard	*L'Interdiction, Illusions perdues, Splendeurs et misères des courtisanes*
Comtesse Ferraud	*Le Colonel Chabert*
Fil-de-Soie	mentioned in *Splendeurs et misères des courtisanes*
Madame Firmiani	*Madame Firmiani*
Colonel Franchessini	*Gobseck*
Princesse Galathionne	mentioned in *Une Fille d'Eve*
Gobseck	*Gobseck, Les Employés, César Birotteau*
Jean-Joachim Goriot	mentioned in *La Maison Nucingen, Modeste Mignon, Splendeurs et misères des courtisanes*
Grandlieu (family)	mentioned in *La Femme abandonnée, La Rabouilleuse*
Comtesse de Kergarouet	*Le Bal de Sceaux*
Duchesse de Langeais	*La Duchesse de Langeais*
Madame de Lanty	*Sarrasine*
Marquise de Listomère	*Etude de femme, La Femme de trente ans*
Comte Henri de Marsay	*Autre Etude de femme, La Fille aux yeux d'or, César Birotteau, Ferragus, La Duchesse de Langeais,* and mentioned in 24 other novels.

Duchesse de Maufrigneuse	*Les Chouans, Le Cabinet des antiques, Splendeurs et misères des courtisanes, Modeste Mignon, Les Secrets de la princesse de Cadignan, Autre Etude de femme*
Baron de Maulincour	*La Duchesse de Langeais, Ferragus*
Michonneau	*Splendeurs et misères des courtisanes*
Montriveau	*La Duchesse de Langeais, Le Lys dans la vallée, Le Contrat de mariage*
Baron de Nucingen	*La Maison Nucingen, Les Employés, La Rabouilleuse, Un Homme d'affaires, Le Député d'Arcis*
Delphine de Nucingen	*César Birotteau, La Maison Nucingen, Le Député d'Arcis*
Poiret	mentioned in *Un Début dans la vie, Splendeurs et misères des courtisanes*
Rastignac (parents)	*Illusions perdues*
Eugène de Rastignac	*Melmoth réconcilié, Illusions perdues, Etude de femme, La Peau de chagrin, L'Interdiction, Le Cabinet des antiques, Le Contrat de mariage, La Maison Nucingen, Une Ténébreuse Affaire, La Cousine Bette*
Laure de Rastignac	*Une Fille d'Eve*
Gabriel de Rastignac	*Le Curé de village*
Comte de Restaud	*Gobseck*
Anastasie de Restaud	*Gobseck, Le Député d'Arcis*
Marquis de Ronquerolles	*Ferragus*; and mentioned in 18 other tales.

When, on sheet 43 of the manuscript, sometime in the autumn of 1834, Balzac crossed out the name Massiac and overwrote it with the name of Rastignac, he did something which forces us to readjust some of the assumptions on which literary study is often based. Does the reappearance of a central character mean that *Old Goriot* is but a chapter of a larger work, *The Human Comedy*, of which Balzac had not yet invented the title or the overall structure? Or does it leave the novel an autonomous entity? *Old Goriot* is clearly both a part of a larger unit, and a unit in itself: you don't need to know about the reappearances (and few readers have memories capacious enough to recall them all in any case) to understand it; but at the same time the reader loses something of the sense of social networks and of the consistency of Balzac's imaginary world if he reads only *Old Goriot*.

The device of the reappearing characters does not entirely destroy the sense of completeness that each novel may possess; but it defers the reader's exhaustion of the novel's interest to the end of *The Human Comedy*, that is to say more or less indefinitely, as *The Human Comedy* has no unambiguous beginning or end.

Obviously, one cannot deal with the question of the aesthetic unity of the individual novels of *The Human Comedy* in quite the same way as with many other novels which, like *Scarlet and Black*, for example, belong to no structure or series outside themselves. Some critics of Balzac's day claimed that the device of the reappearing characters was only invented to allow the novelist to finish his works without having to conclude them. That now seems an unfair accusation; although it is true that the earlier versions of Balzac's novels read by contemporaries (in the case of *Goriot*, III, IV, V and VI) contained more inconsistencies and fewer interconnections than the 'final' version (based on VIII) we now read. By the very design of *The Human Comedy* which *Old Goriot* is the first text to exploit to the full, each of Balzac's novels raises more beginnings than ends on the level of characters and plot. If we take these levels as the ones on which to apply the criterion of completeness, then clearly *Old Goriot* is incomplete, as the adult lives of Victorine, Delphine, Anastasie and Eugène have only just begun; whereas *Scarlet and Black* and *Notre-Dame de Paris*, like any stage tragedy, end with the deaths of their central characters, Julien Sorel and Quasimodo and Esmerelda respectively. Were Goriot himself the sole protagonist of Balzac's novel, then the same would be true of *Old Goriot*; conversely, it is also true that no novelist or tragedian has ever needed to finish off his entire cast in order to create a proper sense of ending. So the special difficulty critics and readers have with Balzac's endings has as much to do with the internal multiplicity of focuses for the plot as with the external multiplicity of connections created by characters reappearing in other texts.

It is important to realise that the multiple narrative focus of *Old Goriot* is one of the principal ways in which Balzac communicates and embodies his vision of the complexity of life. It is not the symptom of indecision (an inability to decide whether he was really writing about Goriot, or Vautrin, or Rastignac), but the fruit of a courageous decision to make the *connectedness* of very different dimensions of social and emotional life the main theme of his novel. The combination of a tragic and foreseeable death with the commencement of a career that will go on beyond the novel's end is precisely the sort of conclusion which is appropriate to a large-scale representation of the interrelatedness of human lives. In a strictly literal, narrative-oriented sense, *Old Goriot* is indeed unfinished; but what this novel aims to represent with as much truthfulness as possible is the unfinishedness of any story about purportedly real people.

In fact, some readers take the view that the structure of *The Human Comedy* reproduces the way in which we know people in real life, seeing them only in parts of their existence and reconstructing a consistent identity from those parts. In this view, what is original and important in the device of the reappearing characters is not so much what we learn about the characters on their reappearance, as the existence of gaps in our knowledge of them, gaps made manifest by the discontinuities between their reappearances. This is certainly one way of enjoying *The Human Comedy*, but it may well make it more 'modern' than Balzac could have imagined. For Balzac, far from wanting to create gaps, struggled with great energy to fill the gaps as they appeared. As we have seen in our account of the manuscript of *Old Goriot*, the device of the reappearing characters itself seems to have arisen as a way of reducing the discontinuities between already-written stories of high society.

Balzac's aim was to be exhaustive, to say everything, to give his fictions the kind of consistency and solidity that belongs (in a different and older way of looking at things) to the real world.

No writer before Balzac had ever created a set of fictions linked in quite the way that the stories of *The Human Comedy* are linked to each other. He certainly owed something to Sir Walter Scott's serial history of Scotland, *The Waverley Novels* (1814–28), which itself harks back to Shakespeare's history plays; but both the British writers order their texts chronologically (*The Human Comedy* has a chronology that cuts across the divisions of the novels) and they allow only historical characters, not fictional ones, to reappear. Of course, many writers of later generations have imitated the design of *The Human Comedy* to a greater or lesser degree: Zola's twenty-novel *Rougon-Macquart* series (1871–92), for example, though it is more limited in scope and uses connections that work in a single direction through the hereditary lineage of a single family, is clearly indebted to Balzac; as are the many *romans-fleuves* of the twentieth century, from Roger Martin du Gard's *Les Thibault* to Louis Aragon's *Les Communistes*. Perhaps the text which most nearly fulfils the Balzacian wager of creating a whole society in all its dimensions in Proust's *A La recherche du temps perdu*; but the model of *The Human Comedy*, whether it is taken to be intentionally, or only incidentally fragmentary, lies behind a host of modern fictional enterprises in forms as diverse as the novel and television serials.

Balzac could not, of course, complete *The Human Comedy*: life is not long enough to say everything; Balzac's life, moreover, was less long than most. But it is fair to say that however long he had worked, there would always have been more connections to make and more stories to weave around the characters and themes of the previous novels. Similarly, every one of Balzac's individual novels, like some kind of living organism, remains susceptible to change and development; as Table 1 shows, every edition of *Old Goriot*, including the last, prompted Balzac to make further amendments. Part of this reluctance to draw the line on a definitive version can be ascribed to the design of *The Human Comedy* which, as it grew, created inconsistencies in names, dates and details in works previously published and which therefore required correction; but another part of it must also be ascribed to Balzac's particular conception of fiction as work *in progress*. His novels do not leave the reader with a sense of an imaginary world closed off to further development, as do – for example – *Scarlet and Black* or Flaubert's *Madame Bovary*. Everything, from the style to the plot, from the connections with other novels to the multiplicity of rewritten versions, can be related to (and, conversely, can be seen as contributing to) the effort to represent and give form to that which has no form, the experience of life as it is lived.

The immediate consequence of changing Massiac to Rastignac was to shift the action of *Old Goriot* from its original date of 1824 to 1819, so that the age of the observer-hero would fit his reappearance as a thirty-year-old in *The Wild Ass's Skin*. As a result, Eugène de Rastignac became an almost exact contemporary of Balzac (born in 1799, aged twenty in the winter of 1819–20, when Rastignac is nineteen) and was transformed, little by little, from a character 'out there' into a possible vehicle for autobiographical reminiscence. It must be stressed that Balzac never sought consciously to write autobiography; and it would be wrong to read *Old Goriot* as a confessional novel in any sense. But as he wrote, Balzac's characters sometimes became alternative selves, as it were, and he gave them, occasionally, attributes, details and experiences that came from his life. In a general sense, Eugène de Rastignac is not like Honoré de Balzac at all; but in some particular senses, Eugène's experiences are almost identical. One case in point is the letter Rastignac receives from his sister: it is very close in tone, and in parts quite close in words, to a letter Balzac wrote to his sister – also called Laure – in 1819 (*Corr* I.30–2).

By the time the first instalments of *Old Goriot* began to appear in the *Revue de Paris* in December 1834, manuscript II of the novel was far from complete. In the course of December and January, Balzac was working furiously on two fronts, correcting the printer's proofs of the earlier parts and composing the later parts at the same time. The last line was written on 26 January 1835, a sentimental anniversary in his relationship with Madame Hanska, and the date he had promised himself to be with her again in Vienna. The last instalment appeared on 11 February; the trip to Vienna was put off until May, so that he would be able to correct the proofs to the book edition which appeared in March, and to the second edition which came out in May.

Proof-reading was a very important part of the habitual way in which Balzac developed his texts. Printers would set his usually very closely-written sheets of handwriting into type, and run off a single 'proof' copy of each page on very large sheets of paper with plenty of room in the margins. These would be returned post-haste to Balzac for the correction of misprints, but the novelist could not reread his own text without making stylistic revisions and often quite substantial additions, which he would scrawl in the margins and link to the printer's text by lines and rings and arrows. What was returned to the printer for resetting looked as though an army of inky-footed spiders had raced across it; such was the difficulty of decipherment that printers' compositors refused to do more than one hour of Balzac each per day. Some writers use the proof stage to delete unnecessary wordage and to hone down their texts; occasional deletions were made by Balzac (mostly in the later stages, that is to say between VI and VIII), but the overwhelming majority of his proof alterations served to fill out his texts with additional material, supplementary detail, and further reflections.

The narrative structure of *Old Goriot*

The fictional world of *Old Goriot* is pretty firmly structured. It is laid out geographically in three distinct and socially separate quarters of nineteenth-century Paris, the Faubourg Saint-

Marceau (on the left bank of the Seine), the Faubourg Saint-Honoré (on the right bank), and the aristocratic Faubourg Saint-Germain (on the left bank, west of the Latin Quarter), with occasional excursions to other areas in the centre (the Ile de la Cité, and the Luxembourg gardens, between the Latin Quarter and the Faubourg Saint-Marceau) and the periphery (the Père Lachaise cemetery, on a hill on the east side of Paris). It is organised hierarchically, into three ranked social spheres, that of the aristocracy (the *salons* of Madame de Beauséant and Anastasie de Restaud), the wealthy bourgeoisie (the Nucingens, the Taillefers), and the mysterious, poverty-stricken rag-bag of the Vauquer lodging-house, which is itself structured vertically in ascending order of poverty. And this fictional world is organised historically, in the telling of a tale that stretches from the origins of Goriot's wealth in the revolutionary disorders of 1792–3 to a perspective of Rastignac's future life from the spring of 1820. These dimensions of order can be constructed quite easily from the novel by the reader, but the reader's only access to them is – obviously enough – through the linear ordering of the text, that is to say from the order in which the stories are actually told. (*The Human Comedy* as a whole has no such linear ordering; there is no more reason to read it in the order of the published volumes than by choosing titles at random.)

The linear order of *Old Goriot* is much less clear than the main structures of the world it depicts or creates. Can it be divided into parts? In writing the manuscript II, Balzac thought of chapter-divisions only in mid-January 1835, and inserted a chapter-title, LA MORT D'UN PÈRE, on sheet 123 (p. 201, after 'ce terrible pronostic'), but crossed it out, only to reinsert it in a different form, LA MORT DU PÈRE on sheet 153 (p. 232, before 'Le lendemain, Rastignac fut éveillé . . .'); and he added an unnumbered sheet at the head of the manuscript giving six chapter-titles, five of which appear for the first time in III where the distinction between 'parts' and 'chapters' remains quite unclear (see p. 15, Table 1). Some modern editions reproduce the chapter divisions of V, which seems the clearest; but Balzac himself did away with them in VI, prior to the deletion of all divisions and many paragraph breaks in all his novels in order to fit them into the sixteen volumes originally planned for VII.

The messy history of the chapter-divisions shows one effect of Balzac's working method on what is traditionally called the structure of the novel. But the uncertainty over the distinction of the parts and the whole is also the trace of the particular kind of novel that *Old Goriot* is. The text puts in necessarily linear order an imagination and a construction that is not linear, but which possesses many simultaneous dimensions which connect up with each other to some extent, but also partly clash. The connections are established and made manifest through the 'mystery' element of the plot and through the explorations of the observer-hero Rastignac; but Balzac also consistently exploits the clashes, or disjunctions, between the different dimensions or levels of his imagined world. Obviously, all attempts, especially Balzac's, to divide a multi-layered construction into satisfactory, linear parts must fail, as any division will leave one dimension or another out of account. Of course that does not mean to say that *Old Goriot* is imperfectly constructed, or lacking in structure. If the novel is to be thought of in these architectural terms of construction or structure, then it would be more appropriate to say that the building blocks or construction units of *Old Goriot* are not easy to define and not fixed in advance; and they are not assembled in order to produce a stable, simple order, but to reproduce in some measure the shifting complexity of human life.

We can now turn back to the narrator, whose presence in the text, commenting on the text, was said (see p. 14) to guarantee the authenticity of the education offered to the reader. In fact, Balzac the narrator withdraws from the telling of his tale for considerable sections of the text. Though his didactic commentary draws out some of the lessons, the story itself is not consistently narrated in his voice, and it would be wrong to assume that just because *Old Goriot* contains an explicit authorial narrator, it is narrated from a single point of view.

To begin with, from the earliest version (II) on, Balzac hands over responsibility for knowledge of the events recounted to the observer–hero, Massiac/Rastignac:

Sans ses observations curieuses et l'adresse avec laquelle il sut se produire dans les salons de Paris, ce récit n'eût pas été coloré des tons vrais qu'il devra sans doute à son esprit sagace et à son désir de pénétrer les mystères d'une situation épouvantable, aussi soigneusement cachée par ceux qui l'avaient créée que par celui qui la subissait.

(pp. 31–2)

(Without his inquiring observations and the skill with which he presented himself in Parisian drawing-rooms, this tale would not have been coloured by the truthful shadings, which it will certainly owe to [Rastignac's] wisdom and to his desire to pierce the mysteries of a frightful situation, as carefully hidden by those who had created it as by him who suffered it.)

The point of view from which this homage is made to Rastignac, like the tenses of the verbs (only a little less curious in French than in my literal rendering) is thoroughly perplexing. On the one hand, it is as if the story *had* already been told, in a manner resembling the narrative framework of other stories published in the *Revue de Paris*, by an older Rastignac, to an amused audience of society ladies appreciating both the figure he cuts and his talent as a story-teller. But that must be nonsense if it is meant to apply to the whole novel: Rastignac would not have cut a dashing figure for long if he had told society ladies of his near-involvement in the murder of Taillefer's son, or of how his flat in the Rue d'Artois had been paid for. (Years later, at a fancy-dress ball narrated in *La Torpille*, a text eventually incorporated into *Splendeurs et misères des courtisanes*, a masked figure takes Rastignac into an embrasure and whispers in his ear: 'What are you living on? Who housed you? Old Goriot! Have you avenged him?' Behind the mask there hides – of course – Vautrin.) On the other hand, it is as if the real story had been already written and based on confidential details given to the novelist by the older Rastignac.

That is more plausible, but it clashes with the first half of the sentence; and the tense of the verb 'qu'il devra' (which it will owe) seems to give away not only the fact that the story has not yet been read, but that it has not yet been *invented*, as was indeed the case in October 1834.

Rastignac could in any event only base a small part of his story on observation, since he meets Goriot in the last months of his life. For all that went before, Rastignac relies on other story-tellers, notably la Duchesse de Langeais, and a figure called Muret who has no other role in this or any other novel than to deliver a biographical portrait of the flour-merchant Jean-Joachim Goriot. Where does *his* information come from? Inside the novel the track stops there; but it may be that the name Muret masks a real-life Marest who may have known a real-life story similar to Goriot's (according to Uffenbeck) and which would explain Balzac's insistence (in prefaces, letters and in other novels) that the story of Goriot was true (see pp. 14, 34). However, the track inside the novel is not designed to give the reader a clear and ordered notion of who said what to whom; it is designed to form a labyrinth, a puzzle, of which only the outer features can be described neatly. As can be seen in Table 3, *Old Goriot* is made up quite substantially of stories told to each other by characters within the story, such that it is impossible, in the last analysis, to say who actually narrates the story of Goriot.

The narrator does not just hand over the role of telling the story to the characters Rastignac, Muret, and so on, but allows them on occasions to take on the function of commenting on the status and nature of their tales. The most striking example is when la Duchesse de Langeais, commenting on her account of Goriot's life, seems to jump into Balzac's own place and offers a new definition of life as drama. In manuscript version II she says:

Ne voyons-nous pas cela tous le jours? Une belle-fille est de la dernière impertinence avec son pauvre beau-père, qui a tout sacrifié pour son

Table 3. *Story-telling in* Old Goriot

Pages	Story	Told by	To
31 on	Goriot's	Rastignac	A Parisian *salon*
63–4	Taillefer's	Mme Couture	Mme Vauquer, Vautrin, Goriot
72	Family history	Rastignac	Comte de Restaud
85–7	Goriot's	Duchesse de Langeais	Rastignac, Mme de Beauséant
88	Delphine's	Mme de Beauséant	Rastignac
94–7	Goriot's	Muret	Rastignac
114	Taillefer's	Vautrin	Rastignac
131–2	Delphine's	Rastignac	Goriot
206–7	Nucingen's deals	Delphine	Goriot, Rastignac
212–13	The diamonds	Anastasie	Goriot, Rastignac, Delphine

fils, un gendre met sa belle-mère à la porte; et nos petits auteurs demandent ce qu'il y a de dramatique aujourd'hui dans la société; mais le drame du gendre est effrayant . . .

(Don't we see that every day? A daughter-in-law is utterly impertinent to her father-in-law, who has sacrificed everything for his son, a son-in-law puts his mother-in-law out in the street; and our little writers wonder whether there's anything dramatic in society nowadays; but the drama of the son-in-law is frightening . . .)

In the final version (VIII) Balzac amends the passage to read 'Ne voyons-nous pas cette tragédie s'accomplissant tous les jours' ('Don't we see this tragedy happening every day'), p. 85, stressing the link between this narrator and the narrator of the attack on the reader on pp. 25–6 of the novel (see pp. 13–14) who is similarly concerned to present daily life in terms of stage drama in general, and tragedy in particular. In this passage, la Duchesse de Langeais becomes a full Balzacian narrator in her own right, that is to say a story-teller making connections between her telling of the tale and the world outside.

In less complex ways, the actual telling of these tales is sometimes as significant in the novel's construction as the tales told. For instance, the snobbery of the aristocracy is held up in front of us by the Duchesse de Langeais's condescending distortion of Goriot's bourgeois name into Doriot, Loriot, Foriot . . . Similarly, Delphine's account of Nucingen's manipulation of her dowry reveals to what extent she participates in the machinery of financial exploitation; and Rastignac's account of Delphine's life to Goriot is designed to show just what a kind heart the young man really has. These are standard uses to which story-tellers put stories told within stories. However, the lop-sided, imperfect embedding of one story in many others is a major feature of the construction of *Old Goriot*, and it can be understood in different ways. In one sense, the paradoxical structure of *Old Goriot* looks back to the eighteenth-century tradition of novels which parody the artificial neatness of conventional plots; in another sense, it also looks forward to more modern scepticism about the reliability of all kinds of knowledge. Thirdly, and least profitably, it can be seen as one of the imperfections deriving from Balzac's hurried working methods. But the indeterminacy of *Old Goriot*'s narrative structure also matches quite precisely the multiple focus of its narrative material and serves, like so many other aspects of this novel, to represent the shifting nature of the life it seeks to recreate.

In *Old Goriot*, linear progression along one or another dimension of the plot is frequently broken off because it is time for dinner (eaten in nineteenth-century France at five o'clock) or for the *déjeuner*, a cross between breakfast and lunch eaten around ten in the morning. Here is a selection of examples of the submission of high society, organised crime, youthful ambition, love and desire to the rumblings of Rastignac's stomach and the raucous calls of the servants Sylvie and Christophe:

p. 64   Madame Couture gives an account of her interview with Taillefer; 'Les pensionnaires, internes et externes, arrivèrent . . .' (The diners, resident and non-resident, arrived . . .')

p. 89   Rastignac leaves Madame de Beauséant. 'Il était cinq heures. Il avait faim . . .' ('It was five o'clock. He was hungry . . .')

p. 105   Vautrin takes Rastignac into the garden to teach him a lesson. Sylvie exclaims 'les voilà qui marchent dans nos artichauts' ('and now they're trampling our artichokes'.) Home-grown artichokes were part of the diet of the Vauquer boarding-house.

p. 167   Rastignac, Goriot and Vautrin are locked in a delicate conversation about Victorine. 'Messieurs, cria Christophe, la soupe vous attend' ('Gentlemen, cried Christophe, soup is on the table').

p. 192   Vautrin has been arrested, Goriot wants to take Rastignac to Delphine. 'Dînons, cria la peintre . . . Par exemple, dit la grosse Sylvie, tout est malheur aujourd'hui, mon haricot de mouton s'est attaché . . .' ('Let's eat, cried the artist . . . What a business, said fat Sylvie, everything's a misfortune today, my bean and mutton stew has stuck to the pan . . .')

p. 199   Madame Vauquer is heartbroken at the loss of so many lodgers. '–Il n'y aura donc que trois tasses de café à faire demain matin, Sylvie' ('So there'll only be three cups of coffee to make tomorrow morning, Sylvie').

p. 249   Thérèse brings news of Delphine to the dying Goriot. 'Vous n'avez plus besoin de moi, faut que j'aille à mon dîner, il est quatre heures et demie' ('You don't need me any more, I must be off to my dinner, it's half past four').

p. 250   Goriot is dead, 'Allons, messieurs, à table' ('Come on, gentlemen, to the dinner-table').

The pangs of hunger and the meal-time interruptions function in *Old Goriot* a little like the chorus in Greek plays, reminding the main actors and the audience of the humbler realities to which they must submit. They are also reminiscent of the comic scenes in Shakespeare's tragedies, which provide an entertaining and realistic low-life counterpoint to the high drama of kings and princes. Alongside these literary echoes,

Balzac's mealtimes also have an important function in allowing the novelist to get out of tight narrative corners, to break off linear progression, to switch from one dimension of his fictional world to another. Because in real life people do eat, and mostly at regular times, the use of mealtimes as narrative shifters could be called realistic. At the same time, one could see Balzac's use of such a realistic feature as mealtimes as a cover for, or 'naturalisation' of, his technical requirement: to interrupt the narrative progression before it runs on too far in any one direction.

The story of how *Old Goriot* was written is a story of growth and change, of a frantic struggle against time in the winter of 1834–5, and of a struggle to complete, adjust and finalise the text over the following ten years. The trace of that struggle is registered in the text in the indeterminate divisions between parts and chapters, in the shifts between its various narrators, and in the sudden jumps between different dimensions – often, but by no means always, covered by a call to eat. Some readers, who feel that a work of art, by some definition they wish to impose, ought to be complete and entire, and demonstrably so, might want to see the way Balzac wrote *Old Goriot* as the reason for its imperfections. Others might feel, as I do, that it is precisely because *Old Goriot* is not a work entirely closed in on itself that it is worth studying with care.

What *Old Goriot* is made from

Balzac lived in the period referred to as the Romantic era in France, when it was often claimed that artistic creation sprang, magically, from the artist's 'genius' or inspiration, rather than from any external source. In a note prefixed to the definitive edition of *Notre-Dame de Paris* in 1832, Balzac's contemporary, the poet, playwright and novelist Victor Hugo (1802–85) expressed the Romantic notion of artistic creativity thus:

Novels . . . are born, in a way that is in some sense necessary, with all their chapters; dramas are born with all their scenes . . . Once the thing is done, don't change your mind, don't touch it any more. Once the book is published, once the work's sex – manly or otherwise – has been established and declared, once the infant has given its first cry, it is born, that's all there is to it, that's the way it's come out, father and mother can neither of them do anything more about it.

Balzac's attitude to his work was radically different from Hugo's typically Romantic (and, in the specific case of *Notre-Dame de Paris*, somewhat dishonest) glorification of the inspired writer's creation of masterpieces whole and entire at the first draft. For Balzac, writing was comparable to childbirth not as the instantaneous creation of new life, but as something delivered after long gestation and protracted labour. He did not claim to conceive the plots and characters of his novels easily, or by the sole working of his imagination or inspiration. He claimed to take his material from life, from the observation of the reality around him:

As for the whole set of facts reported . . . all are true, taken singly, even the most novel-like . . . No human head would be powerful enough to invent such a large number of tales, is it not then a great feat just to be able to put them all together.

(from the preface to *Le Cabinet des Antiques* (1839), *Pl* IV.962–3)

The central story of *Old Goriot*, of an old man left to die in poverty by daughters he had made wealthy, was, Balzac insisted, a 'true' story which he had adapted and toned down to make more credible as a fiction:

The event used as a model [for *Le Père Goriot*] presented frightful circumstances, of a sort you wouldn't find amongst Cannibals; the poor father cried out for water, for the whole twenty hours of his death agony, without anyone coming to his aid . . . That kind of truth wouldn't have been credible.

(from the preface to *Le Cabinet des Antiques*, *Pl* IV.962)

It is not just Balzac the novelist, speaking in his own voice in prefaces and introductions, but also Balzac's fictional characters who insist that the Goriot story is 'true'. This has a mildly paradoxical effect; when the fictional Derville recalls that he has seen 'a father die in an attic, without a farthing, abandoned by two daughters he'd given forty thousand francs' income to . . .', the 'true' story of Goriot becomes, once again, a literary fiction of truth in the mind of a character in a novel. But the lawyer Derville, in this passage added to *Le Colonel Chabert* in 1835, is really being used as the novelist's mouthpiece when he adds that 'In the end, all the horrors that novelists think they have invented are always less than the truth' (*Pl* III.373).

The horrors invented in *Old Goriot*, whether or not they are a modified version of a real-life story known to Balzac (and they may well be: see Uffenbeck), are also quite close to the material of several prior literary texts. In the first scene of Shakespeare's *King Lear* (1606), an ageing monarch, having decided to divide his kingdom between his children, asks each of his three daughters to say how much they love him so he may decide what part of his wealth they deserve. Two daughters, Goneril and Regan, respond with fulsome praise of the old man; but from the third, Cordelia, comes only one word, 'Nothing'. The King warns her: 'Nothing will come of nothing: speak again'. Lear's words could be taken as a motto for the study of all works of literature, and *Old Goriot* is no exception to the rule that all books are made from something, and always made in some part from other books. Indeed, the sentence Shakespeare gave to Lear he took from the *Satires* of the Latin poet Persius: 'Nothing can come of nothing, nothing can go back to nothing', ('De nihilo nihilum, in nihilum nil posse reverti'), *Satires* I.84. *Old Goriot*, for its part, seems to come, distantly, from *Lear*: both works deal with a father giving all his wealth to daughters who then reject him.

The obvious and significant difference between the central plots of *Lear* and *Goriot* is the absence, in Balzac's version, of the third daughter, Cordelia, the uncompromising, good and loving daughter. Her role is taken over (and altered beyond easy recognition) by Rastignac, who is neither a girl, nor a descendent of the protagonist, nor unambiguously good. This fundamental alteration prompted a critic of Balzac's day, Saint-Marc Girardin, to claim that *Old Goriot* was an 'immoral' and inferior version of *Lear*, lacking the positive moral weight of a Cordelia to contrast with the unalloyed wickedness of Delphine/Goneril and Anastasie/Regan. It is wrong to think that the absence of virtue personified makes *Old Goriot* immoral as a novel, for Balzac has other ways of referring back to the older values; but it is certainly true that the world he represents is a sombre one even in comparison to Shakespeare's, and even more so when set beside another play dealing with a very similar theme, *Les Deux Gendres* (1810), by Charles-Guillaume Etienne (1777–1845). Balzac certainly knew Etienne's play (much appreciated by the novelist Stendhal and praised for its modern seriousness in his pamphlet on *Racine et Shakespeare* (1824)), just as certainly as he and Etienne both knew a tale by Gayot de Pitaval, first published in 1760, which was itself very close to *Conaxa*, a story (whose eighteenth-century Jesuit author remains unknown) telling of a wealthy tradesman of Antwerp who gave his daughters huge dowries on their marriages and retired from business, only to find his daughters and sons-in-law turn thankless and spiteful towards him. Unlike Lear or Goriot, Jean Conaxa gets his own back by tricking his sons-in-law into believing he still has a fortune in his strong-box. Etienne's play also has a morally satisfying outcome.

The existence of these quite similar prior texts (*Conaxa* can be read in Barbéris, pp. 53–5) does not necessarily contradict Balzac's claim that the central material of *Old Goriot* is 'true'. The original, real-life story may have appealed to Balzac as suitable literary material (and may have been readable as literature by the public) precisely because it corresponded sufficiently to known literary models. The similarity of the story to *King Lear* predisposes the reader to perceive the novel's tragic dimension; its likeness to Etienne's *drame bourgeois* may account for Balzac's particular stress on the middle-class setting. The 'sources' of *Old Goriot* are in the end as important for the comparisons, contrasts, allusions and echoes that they bring to the reader as for the (limited) contribution they make to understanding how Balzac put the novel together.

'Real life' and literature are not the only two types of source material that Balzac made use of in composing *Old Goriot*. As might be expected in a text which marks the emergence of the concept of *The Human Comedy* with its myriad interconnections of characters, plots and settings, it also draws for its material on stories and themes worked out differently in other Balzacian texts. Finally, and again as might be expected, Balzac's reworking and repetition of material takes place not only *between* different novels written at different times, but also *within* individual works. *Old Goriot* repeats other Balzac stories; up to a point, it also repeats itself. As these internal sources function in much the same way as the external sources from the point of view of the reader, it seems proper to treat them similarly as part of what the novel is made from.

The parable of the mandarin is put by Eugène de Rastignac to his fellow-student Horace Bianchon on p. 134 to make his own moral dilemma clearer to himself. He wants to know if a crime – the proposed murder of Victorine Taillefer's brother – can be justified. He connects his difficult situation to the moral concerns of eighteenth-century French philosophy by saying that his parable comes from Jean-Jacques Rousseau (1712–78). In fact it does not; its true source has been tracked down (by Ronai) in Chateaubriand's *Génie du christianisme* (1802), which Rastignac quotes explicitly in a different connection on p. 172, where it reads:

If by a mere wish you could kill a man in China and inherit his fortune in Europe, with the supernatural certainty that no-one would ever know anything about it, would you consent to forming that wish?

Balzac's misattributed version is copied quite closely: Rastignac asks his honest medical friend if he remembers the passage where 'Rousseau' asks his reader 'what he would do in a situation where, without shifting from Paris, he was able to grow rich by killing an old mandarin in China, by his willpower alone'. Bianchon decides, like Chateaubriand, that you should leave the Chinaman alone, and Rastignac is much relieved: outright crime, even if kept secret, is not right. But this cannot be seen by Balzac's reader as the final answer to the problem: the novelist's world is haunted by the dilemma, by the parable (which had in fact been used before, without attribution, and with 'New-Holland' replacing China, in one of Balzac's earliest novels, *Annette et le criminel*, written in collaboration and published under the name of Horace de Saint-Aubin in 1824), and above all by stories of men who acted on the other possible answer to Rastignac's (or Chateaubriand's) question. In the text of *Old Goriot*, Vautrin gives the opposite answer as if it were a fact of history:

The secret of great fortunes with no visible source is a crime forgotten because it was neatly done. (p. 116)

However, Vautrin's answer is only one version, reduced to a maxim or sentence, of a story that recurs through Balzac's writing and in *Old Goriot* itself. In 1831, the novelist published the first version of a tale, 'L'Auberge rouge', dealing with a character then named Mauricey whose great wealth stems from the murder of a chance acquaintance long ago. Also in 1831, in a major novel, *The Wild Ass's Skin*, Balzac set a banquet scene in the home of a wealthy financier about whom 'envious people and those keen to perceive the mechanisms of life' say:

this man is supposed to have killed, during the Revolution, some old asthmatic woman, a scrofulous little orphan, and some other person. (*Pl* X.1258, note c).

In 1834, Balzac puts into *Old Goriot* a stony-hearted father, the millionaire financier Taillefer. Again according to the all-knowing Vautrin, 'il passe pour avoir assassiné un de ses amis pendant la Révolution' ('he is held to have murdered one of his friends during the Revolution'), p. 114. Thus the mandarin tale comes from outside the text (from Chateaubriand, alias Rousseau); it also comes (with modification) from one of Balzac's pseudonymous early works, *Annette et le criminel*, and illuminates a tale told in 'L'Auberge rouge', *The Wild Ass's Skin*, and in *Old Goriot* itself, where the parable serves to mirror the episodes which, conversely, give it narrative substance. Origin and function are almost inextricably interwoven. Balzac sought to tighten the knots of his text even further, by renaming the Mauricey of 'L'Auberge rouge' and the financier of *The Wild Ass's Skin*. In versions rewritten and published after *Old Goriot*'s first appearance, both are called Taillefer.

'La Femme abandonnée' is the title of a tale first published in 1832 in the *Revue de Paris* (in which *Goriot* was also first published, see p. 7) which tells of the desertion of Madame de Beauséant by her lover Gaston de Nueil. In the 1832 story, this is not the first time she has suffered a lover's rejection; but the story of that *prior* heartbreak is not told (or invented) until the writing of *Old Goriot* in 1834. So, like the mandarin story, the 'deserted woman' is a recurrent Balzacian plot-type, and its recurrence in *Goriot* can be seen as another pointer to the internal constitution of the novel out of Balzac's set of personal themes belonging neither entirely to life nor entirely to books. Moreover, the theme of the rejected or deserted woman does not appear in *Old Goriot* uniquely in the story of Madame de Beauséant. In the winter of 1819–20, when the action takes place, (i) Delphine de Nucingen is deserted by her lover de Marsay, (ii) la duchesse de Langeais is abandoned by her lover Montriveau and (iii) Victorine Taillefer is abandoned by a young man she has begun to regard as her sweetheart if not her lover, Eugène de Rastignac. The novel feeds upon itself, as well as feeding upon Balzac's personal stock of themes, situations and character-types, upon the themes and situations of European literature, and on material taken from life and French history. The repetition within the novel of the 'deserted lover' functions as an element of the novel's form, or structure; but that internal repetition is not clearly different from the rep-

etition in *Old Goriot* of the story of Madame de Beauséant from
'La Femme abandonnée' written two years earlier.

The last example given is more usually treated as part of the
form or structure of *Old Goriot* rather than as a special kind of
material or source. The distinction between material and form
is of course part of the machinery of criticism, not part of the
novel: Balzac's design, like the design of all but parodic and
modern, self-conscious novelists, is to obscure the source of his
material without losing the allusive power those sources may
possess, and to mask the form so that the material appears to
present a certain kind of experience directly. It seems to me that
in *Old Goriot* Balzac achieved at least these aims sufficiently
fully to make critical distinctions between material and form
somewhat arbitrary; the device of repetition is not very
obviously different when it is applied to *King Lear* and when it is
applied to the theme of the abandoned lover. To study this
novel's form involves, obligatorily, some knowledge of where
its material comes from; and, conversely, the novel's sources
should be thought of in terms of the roles they play in the
novel's form.

Old Goriot is by no means an easy text to read, and much of its
difficulty stems from its unusually dense network of cultural
reference and allusion. Balzac puts several dozen poets,
playwrights, composers, novelists and writers, of Greek, Latin,
English, Scottish, Italian and French origin, into his text, in
ways that are worth detailed consideration. The overall effect,
for some readers, is one of wilful obscurity; for others, of
erudite showmanship (see Lock's comment, p. 14); but
Balzac's cultural baggage is also of fascinating complexity, and
serves to bind lived experience and literary memory, the real
world and the world of books, into an inextricable whole.

One major function of cultural reference in *Old Goriot* is to
give substance to the historical moment in which the action is
set, to fulfil the aim of writing a history of life as it is lived, on the
assumption that life is not just a matter of eating but also an

experience of culture. In the course of Balzac's lifetime, and outside of the recognised domains of high culture, great efforts were made to find new and more authentic ways of representing what the eye can see – efforts that would culminate in the invention of photography by Daguerre in 1838–9. One of the stages in Daguerre's development was the Diorama, a display of coloured two-dimensional cardboard figures in a three-dimensional space, in which controlled lighting was used to impart an illusion of movement to the scene. The young Balzac thought it one of 'merveilles du siècle', ('wonders of the age') (*Corr* I.205), and he lends the younger boarders at the Vauquer lodging house his own early enthusiasm (pp. 64ff.) as part of his memory of what it was like to be living in Paris at that time. In fact, a slight anachronism is involved. The Diorama opened on 11 July 1822, thirty months after the conversation at Madame Vauquer's dinner-table. When these early sheets of the manuscript were written, the law student was still called Massiac and the action was set in 1824. When Massiac was turned into Rastignac and the date shifted back to 1819 (see p. 23), Balzac could not alter the Diorama references, built into the whole linguistic comedy of the dinner-table.

The Diorama places the poor and the young in the (slightly telescoped) historical–cultural moment. The music of Rossini (1792–1868) fulfils the same 'placing' function for the wealthier characters, and in particular for Delphine de Nucingen. She has a box at the Théâtre des Italiens, and takes Rastignac to see *The Barber of Seville* (1816), first performed in Paris to wild acclaim on 26 October 1819. The dating, here, is remarkably accurate; and the enthusiasm of Rastignac ('Je n'avais jamais entendu de si délicieuse musique', ('I never heard such exquisite music'), p. 133) accurately reflects Parisian attitudes in the period: Rossini was appointed Director of the Théâtre des Italiens in 1824, where he stayed until he lost his job in the political upheavals of 1830.

But Rossini does not just belong to the 'background', the set of references smuggled in, so to speak, to lend historical authenticity to the lives of fictional characters. His operas are also appropriated by Delphine and used in her sentimental liaison with Rastignac. At a performance of *Moses in Egypt* (1810: first performed in Paris on 20 October 1822; another slight anachronism) Rastignac is moved to adopt what now seems a rather hollow, Romantic musical posture: 'Pour les uns c'est une même note, pour les autres c'est l'infini de la musique', ('For some people it's a single note, for others it's the whole of music'), p. 225 (but see Balzac's long expansion of this view of *Moses in Egypt* in *Massimila Doni*, written in 1837). In her letter begging Rastignac to come to her in time for the Beauséant ball, Delphine throws this appreciation of Rossini back at Eugène, transferring its reference to the sentimental domain. 'I'm sure', she writes, 'that you are faithful to me despite all the different shades of feeling between us. It's like what you said when listening to Rossini . . .' Culture here becomes a weapon in personal conflict; but it does not cease to be a cultural reference, signalling (to us, but also to Rastignac and to Delphine herself) not only that her life is lived in a certain social sphere (of wealth), but in and through the imagination.

As the wealthy went to the Italiens for Rossini and to the Opéra for Cimarosa (Anastasie de Restaud is practising a line from *Il matrimonio segreto* on the piano when Rastignac calls, p. 74), the less well-off flocked in the first few years of peace for a generation to the vaudevilles, melodramas and comic operas performed mostly in theatres on the Boulevard du Temple – also known as the 'boulevard du crime' – where, amongst the throng of theatre audiences, pickpockets and the perpetrators of more serious crimes plied their trades. Vautrin must have spent a lot of time there, because he remembers: (a) a comic opera by Nicolo and Etienne, *Joconde ou les coureurs d'aventure* (1814), from which he sings 'J'ai longtemps parcouru le monde . . .' on pp. 56, 57, 167; (b) an opera by Boieldieu and Godard d'Ancour de Saint-Just, *Le Calife de Bagdad* (1800, but still performed in 1819), to which he refers on p. 157 (*Il Buondocani* is the name under which the Caliph Isauun goes around Baghdad at night); (c) a comedy with music adapted from Dufresny by J.-B. Vial, *Les Deux Jaloux* (1813), from which he sings 'Ma Fanchette est charmante . . .' on pp. 163, 186; (d) an eighteenth-century comic opera by Grétry and Sedaine, *Richard Cœur de Lion*, from which he sings a refrain adopted by the royalists in the revolutionary period, 'O Richard, ô mon roi', on p. 167; (e) a pantomime by Balison de Rougemont, *La Femme innocente, malheureuse et persécutée, ou L'Epoux crédule et barbare* (1811), of which he misquotes the title on p. 58; and he must have just seen (f) a vaudeville by Scribe (who had worked alongside Balzac as a lawyer's apprentice for a short while in 1817) and Delavigne, *La Somnambule*, first performed on 6 December 1819, from which he sings 'Dormez, mes chères amours . . .' on p. 171.

Madame Vauquer takes the tuneful Vautrin as a jolly and cultivated fellow, and is delighted (on pp. 170–1) to be invited by him to see the current star actor of melodrama, Marty, in *Le Solitaire*, a highly popular but utterly second-rate Pixérécourt play, based on a pot-boiling novel by the vicomte d'Arlincourt (but actually launched in 1821: another minor time-shift), which she has manifestly not read though she says she has ('que nous aimions tant à lire', ('which we so loved reading'), p. 171) because she attributes it to 'Atala de Chateaubriand', a comic mishmash of François-René de Chateaubriand (see p. 36) and his celebrated semi-confessional romance of love in the American wilds, *Atala* (1801).

Madame Vauquer, like a French Mrs Malaprop, misappropriates high culture, but lives no less than the other characters in a world that is full of books. Bianchon brings out a line from Virgil's *Bucolics*, no doubt learned at school (p. 191), Rastignac sees Madame de Beauséant in terms of Homer's *Iliad* (p. 230) and himself as Cherubino (from Mozart's *Marriage of Figaro*, p. 126), whilst Madame de Beauséant sees herself as Rastignac's Ariadne in the Minoan labyrinth of Paris (p. 89); even Laure de Rastignac flaunts her culture by adapting a line from Corneille's *Cinna* on p. 101. Vautrin seizes upon literature

and uses it to project the image of a man who has, in the words
of the song, 'longtemps parcouru le monde . . .', ('long travel-
led the world'), and has learnt a thing or two: 'J'ai lu les
mémoires de Benvenuto Cellini . . . et en italien encore', ('I've
read the memoirs of Benvenuto Cellini [Italian sculptor,
1500–71, gives information on power struggles and personal
affairs of rulers in sixteenth-century Rome, Florence and
Paris] . . . and in Italian at that!' p. 107; see also Vautrin's use
of Italian on p. 179). Vautrin also uses references to historical
figures in the same way (La Fayette, and Talleyrand by
implication, p. 115) but it is literature which makes it possible
for him to reveal the deepest secrets of life:

Eh bien! pour moi qui ai bien creusé la vie, il n'existe qu'un seul
sentiment réel, une amitié d'homme à homme. Pierre et Jaffier, voilà
ma passion. Je sais *Venise sauvée* par cœur.   (p. 155)

(Well! for me, and I've really got to the bottom of life, there's only one
real feeling that exists, and that's friendship between man and man.
Pierre and Jaffier, that's my passion. I know *Venice Preserv'd* by heart.)

Thomas Otway's tragedy of 1682 (which was itself based on an
earlier text by César de Saint-Réal, 1639–92) tells of Jaffier's
'exalted friendship' for an enemy soldier. Balzac's use of
reference to this English play does not just serve, like the
similarity of the Goriot story to *King Lear*, to connect the novel
to the language of Shakespeare and to the 'noble' genre of
tragedy (pp. 13–14). It helps us also to see Vautrin's attempt to
impose himself on the younger man as, amongst other things,
an attempt to establish his own cultural superiority, and, in this
respect, Vautrin's Otway allusion mirrors the functioning of the
narrator's cultural allusions more generally with respect to the
reader. But it is also fairly clear that Vautrin (and presumably
Balzac) believe Jaffier's 'exalted friendship' to be a dramatic
euphemism for homosexuality, and French readers have traditionally assumed that what Vautrin means to tell Rastignac is
that he is at least a potential lover of the younger man. If that is
so, then the phrase 'Je sais *Venise sauvée* par cœur' offers the

reader a model of the use to which reading literature can be put: namely, to make oneself comprehensible to others, as a tool of communication which confirms participation in a shared culture.

Some of the literary references and allusions in *Old Goriot* are not part of any character's speech and belong directly to the narrative, or to the narrator, whose range is much the same as his characters' – from Latin poetry (the satires of Juvenal, p. 37) to English literature (Byron, p. 199), to late eighteenth-century comedy (Doliban, p. 95 and p. 164, is from *Le Sourd ou l'Auberge pleine*, by Choudart-Desforges). Most of the uses of literary allusion by the narrator are as two-edged as those of the characters: they serve both to communicate (saying that Vautrin's witticisms were worthy of Juvenal tells the reader what they were like, if s/he has read Juvenal) and to communicate that the narrator knows Juvenal, that is to say to assert cultural superiority. However, there is another use to which Balzac puts literature in *Old Goriot*, and that is to say what Rastignac and his world are not like. In modern times, he writes on p. 128, one no longer comes across 'ces hommes rectangulaires, ces belles volontés qui ne plient jamais', ('those square men, those strong wills that never bend') of the sort Molière wrote about in *Le Misanthrope*, and Sir Walter Scott, in *Heart of Midlothian*. The narrator then moves on, by the force of his argument, to suggest that one could write a work no less fine than Molière's and no less dramatic, on the opposite material. The opposite would be the depiction of 'les sinuosités dans lesquelles un homme du monde, un ambitieux fait rouler sa conscience', ('the crooked lines of society around which a man of the world, a man of ambition, contorts his conscience'). Indeed one could – for this passage occurs *within* the very work that it calls for, a depiction of a man of ambition bending his conscience to the devious ways of Parisian society.

In this passage, which seems to aim initially only to set the literary boundaries of his subject, Balzac slips – perhaps inadvertently, perhaps unwittingly – into a *representation* of the novel within the novel, a device much used by twentieth-century novelists and story-tellers such as André Gide (in *The Counterfeiters*), Jorge Luis Borgès and Georges Perec (whose *Life: A User's Manual* (1978), like *Old Goriot*, weaves many tales around the inhabitants of a single Parisian apartment house). Obviously, self-representation of this kind (technically known as *mise en abyme*, and most easily understood in the visual domain, such as in those paintings of artists painting pictures of an artist painting, etc.) is not often found in novels which seek primarily to persuade readers that what is represented in them is life, not art. But this instance of *mise en abyme* in *Old Goriot*, set alongside the novel's opening discussion of its own status as not a novel but something else (*drame*, *histoire*, 'true') as well as the bursts of stylistic humour, show, amongst other things, that Balzac's particular brand of realism is not entirely incompatible (as Flaubert's or Theodor Fontane's would be in later decades of the nineteenth century) with the eighteenth-century tradition of the parodic novel; and it can also serve to remind us, by way of conclusion to our study of what *Old Goriot* is made from, of how much in this realistic representation of Parisian social life actually emerges from the cultural and literary sources and allusions woven into its fabric.

Chapter 2

The achievement of Old Goriot

The representation of social life

One of the things that *Old Goriot* does for many readers is to create the illusion of life. To make the reader or listener or spectator 'suspend his disbelief' and to enter a representation as it if were the life represented has been the aim of a long tradition of writers and artists from antiquity to the present. The history of *mimesis*, or representation, is told, amongst others, by Auerbach and Levin, and for both of these critics *Old Goriot* is a landmark in the development of modern ways of writing realistically. If Balzac does succeed in creating the illusion of real life for his reader, he does it by means that are significantly different from Victor Hugo's highly-coloured, intensely visual descriptions of medieval Paris in *Notre-Dame de Paris*, just as they are different from Flaubert's impersonal and impassive approach to the miseries of provincial life in *Madame Bovary* (1857). However, the creation of a fleeting effect of 'lifelikeness' is not at all rare in literature and art, and one of the more curious aspects of cultural history is to discover what past generations took to be *vraisemblable* or lifelike. As a young man, Balzac himself was an enthusiastic admirer even of Daguerre's old cardboard Diorama (p. 40).

Daguerre and Bouton have amazed the whole of Paris; a thousand problems are solved since in front of a canvas screen you believe you're in a church a hundred yards from each thing. It's the wonder of the age.
(*Corr* I.205)

Whether or not a representational work of high or low art creates an illusion of real life obviously depends not only on the artist's skill, but also on the viewer's or reader's wish or need to

46

be taken in, and just as obviously also on what he or she is accustomed to allowing him or herself to be taken in by. General discussion of the 'reality-effect' of *Old Goriot*, or of any other novel, must therefore be set in the context of readers' expectations, experiences, habits and so forth – expectations of what novels are like, on the one hand, but also expectations about life, on the other.

What is of course unusual about *Old Goriot* is not that it enthralled readers of the 1830s with a representation that could be taken to be just like life, but that a century and a half later it still has the power to convince readers of its truthfulness. Our expectations and experiences of what novels are like are different from those of Balzac's original audience; but the impact of *The Human Comedy* on the subsequent course of the European novel means that our expectations are themselves in part indirectly formed by *Old Goriot* itself. What marked Balzac's manner in particular, and what distinguishes it especially from the historical and romantic novels of its own era, is the stress it lays on the role of money in social life, the prominence it gives to material objects in everyday life, and the way it locates its characters in a very precise and contemporary setting. These features must have lost some of the impact of newness that they had in the 1830s; but they have not lost their ability to create a powerful impression of life as it really was.

In *Old Goriot*, Balzac assumes that you need money to live on; and that people think about their income, expenditure and balance for much of their waking lives. Such a view of life as the management of finance fits the common culture of twentieth-century readers, governed for the most part by politicians who dress up all issues as questions of economics, rather better than the attitudes of a nineteenth-century audience, for whom religious, moral and political considerations played a large conscious role in decisions about life. Thus the way in which Balzac tracks the financial fortunes of Goriot, Anastasie, Delphine and Eugène de Rastignac must have different effects on different readers. If, for example, like the elegant readers the

Revue de Paris pretended it served, you have been told, perhaps, that money matters less than breeding, faith and monarchy, and is in any case not to be mentioned in society, then you are likely to find *Old Goriot* not merely impolite but also unrealistic. If, however, you suspect that money matters much more than – let us say – your family will admit, then Balzac's novel may seem to be a bewildering revelation of how life really works, and may alter your perception of your own life. But if you already share the view put by Goriot that 'monnaie fait tout', ('money does everything'), p. 208, then the novel may seem merely realistic in the emphasis it puts on financial matters. The second type of reader is certainly the one on whom *Old Goriot* is designed to make the greatest impact, and it is designed to educate such a reader into the attitude of the third type. Money constitutes a major and quite specific feature of the world depicted in *Old Goriot*: to understand that world properly (and irrespective of whether one thinks it is, or is really like, the real world), the reader needs to understand how money functions in the novel.

Old Goriot shows how one man can lose a fortune, and how another, younger man (but not women: see p. 50) can learn to survive without one. In the early 1800s, the pile extracted by Goriot from the grain trade must have reached at least 1,200,000 francs, because he has enough invested (in *rentes*, the nineteenth-century equivalent of Treasury stock, which paid 4–5 per cent annual interest throughout the period) to produce an income of 60,000 francs p.a. (p. 96). But his capital must have been over 2,000,000 francs by 1808, when his daughters marry, because he gives each of them a dowry of about a million francs ('50.000 fr. de rente', see p. 16; 'quarante mille livres de rente', see p. 34; 'ton bon petit million', *Old Goriot*, p. 208), leaving himself about 200,000 francs invested in the *Grand Livre* of undated Government stock which produces – as Madame Vauquer's prying eyes and mental arithmetic reveal – an income of 'about eight to ten thousand francs' (p. 39) when Goriot finally retires from business in 1813 and comes to live at the

Table 4. *French currency units in 1819*

maille, liard	Obsolete, demonetised coins of no value; proverbially, 'a farthing'
sou	Obsolete coin, equivalent to 5 centimes; used for calculations
centime	Smallest currency unit
franc	100 centimes or 20 sous
livre	1 franc, names used interchangeably
écu	3 francs
Louis	12 francs
Napoléon	1 Louis, names used interchangeably.
Louis d'or, Napoléon d'or	24 francs

boarding-house. He pays his landlady 1,200 francs a year for his first-floor room and full board at this stage; the margin between income and expenditure is very handsome. But over the following six years to 1819 he parts with most of the capital, 'mille francs à mille francs', ('thousand by thousand'), according to Delphine (p. 214), to pay the debts of his daughter Anastasie's playboy lover, Maxime de Trailles. By December 1819, all he has left is about 27,000 francs, of which he spends 12,000 on buying and furnishing the flat in the rue d'Artois for Delphine's lover, Rastignac, and with the remainder he buys an annuity (*rente viagère*, payable only up to death, the capital sum being lost to heirs) of 1,200 francs per annum (p. 214). This means that Maxime de Trailles has spent and gambled away the best part of a quarter of a million francs during his liaison with Anastasie ('plus de deux cent mille francs', according to Delphine, p. 215) – about 170,000 francs coming through Anastasie from Goriot, and something less than 100,000 francs ('Les diamants n'ont pas été vendus cent mille francs', p. 213) from the illegal sale of the Restaud family diamonds to the usurer Gobseck: 'the family diamonds Monsieur de Restaud is so attached to, his diamonds, mine, everything, I sold the lot' (p. 212). Restaud buys the diamonds back. Strictly speaking he

Table 5. *Laws of marriage in nineteenth-century France (from the* Code civil*)*

Article 213	Le mari doit protection à sa femme, la femme obéissance à son mari (The husband owes his wife protection, the wife owes obedience to her husband)
Article 215	La femme ne peut ester en jugement sans l'autorisation de son mari (The wife cannot testify in court without her husband's authority)

Two types ('régimes') of marriage contract were possible. Under the 'régime de la communauté des biens' the married couple jointly owned all that both parties possessed on marriage, including the bride's dowry. Under the 'régime de la séparation des biens', used for both Anastasie's and Delphine's marriages, what the bride possessed on marriage, including her dowry, remained legally separate from her husband's property. But the following dispositions made the distinction (on which Goriot desperately insists, p. 207) largely inoperable:

Article 1421	Le mari administre seul les biens de la communauté. Il peut les vendre, aliéner et hypothéquer sans le concours de sa femme (The husband administers the common assets alone. He may sell, dispose of and mortgage them without his wife's involvement)
Article 217	La femme, même non commune ou séparée de biens, ne peut donner, aliéner, hypothéquer, acquérir à titre gratuit ou onéreux, sans le concours du mari dans l'acte, ou son consentement par écrit (The wife, even if married under a contract of separation of assets, may not give, dispose of, mortgage, or acquire goods whether or not any obligation is involved, without her husband's signature on the deed or his agreement in writing)

would only have been entitled to use Anastasie's dowry to do this (see Table 5, Article 1421) if he married her under the 'régime de la communauté'; so instead he uses his wife's scandalous theft of family property to blackmail her into promising to sign over all her dowry to his name (p. 213). And that is how a million francs originally extracted from the starving revolutionaries of 1793 ends up in the hands of . . . a hereditary aristocrat.

Goriot's other million is deviously appropriated by the crooked financier Nucingen. He does not steal the money but invests it under his wife's name (thus respecting the law under which he administers but does not own Delphine's dowry) in shady deals which will result in it being technically lost, but regained many times over by companies which Nucingen runs in his own name (the details are given on p. 209). It's not clear whether Balzac copied Nucingen's swindle from life; but it's certain that many have copied Nucingen into life – though with changes in marriage and tax laws his most faithful imitators reverse his procedure nowadays and put the company's money in the wife's name.

Vautrin's plot to murder Taillefer's son in order to gain 200,000 francs in commission looks quite modest in this context, and thus even more bizarre. He wants the money, he says, to set himself up on a plantation in the New World, with two hundred slaves. *Old Goriot* allows us to work out some of the human values of nineteenth-century society in numbers: for one playboy lover, a quarter of a million francs in running costs alone; for one American negro, including the land he will work on, one thousand francs outright.

The minimum budget for a single person in Paris in 1819 was one hundred francs per month – that is what Goriot leaves himself to live on (p. 196) and what Rastignac gets by way of regular support from his family (p. 108). Nearly half (forty-five francs, p. 31) goes on the cheapest available bed and board. But even that bare minimum represents an enormous sacrifice for gentry whose income derives solely from agriculture; specifically, viticulture: 'le produit tout industriel de la vigne', ('the product of the vine which has to be worked for every penny') and does not total more than 3,000 francs for a family of seven (see *Goriot*, p. 49 for details). The cash-flow of Parisian lives is simply huge compared to the economy of the countryside, and to the regular salaries paid by the State to its officials. Against the 3,000 franc income that could be earned from working a vineyard, or the 3,000 franc salary of a 'procureur du roi' (public prosecutor), p. 109, Rastignac needed to spend 12,000 francs a year just to live as a barrister in Paris, according to Vautrin, and 25,000 francs a year to keep up appearances as a fashionable dandy (p. 109). Delphine's dowry gives her an unearned income equivalent to the earnings of the half-dozen top lawyers in the capital (p. 109), at around 50,000 francs a year. The ratio from the bottom to the top of the scale of incomes specified in *Old Goriot*, at 1:41, is more likely to be found today in the developing countries than in the West; and the leap Rastignac wants to make from genteel rural poverty to lavish urban elegance is a formidably long one. How does he do it?

Balzac never solved the problem for himself, and might not have written *Old Goriot* if he had. Consequently, his novel is necessarily vague on what might be considered a key issue in debates about his realism. Rastignac obtains 1,550 francs by blackmailing his mother's feelings (for 1,200, by threatening suicide, p. 92), and by tapping his sisters' loyalty and savings (for 350, pp. 99–101). This enables him to open accounts with tailors and bootmakers and glovemakers and the other suppliers of the 'tools with which you spade the vine in this corner of the world' (p. 92), and to live on credit. He acquires a further 1,000 by magic when he gambles Delphine's 100 franc stake up to 7,000 at his first-ever splash at the roulette-wheel (p. 140): she takes back only the 6,000 needed to pay off her ex-lover de Marsay. But for the rest, Rastignac lives on unspecified gambling wins, on credit, and on air: with his gambling wins he buys watches and gold chains which he then pawns at the Mont-de-piété ('the state-run pawn office, that dark and discreet friend of youth', p. 148), presumably for the cash stake for his next game of roulette. If applied systematically, this procedure would result either in Rastignac owning a great number of watches which he would not have the cash to redeem from pawn, or, if he lost at roulette, a smaller number of un-redeemable timepieces. It's as nonsensical as Balzac's plan to solve his own financial problems by reopening Roman silver mines in Sardinia (see Maurois, pp. 372–8) or by marrying an aristocratic widow subject to the rules on export of capital laid down by the Tsar of Russia (see Maurois, p. 553). And of course, Rastignac couldn't pay Madame Vauquer with pawn-tickets:

his daring deserted him as did his conjuring ability when he had to face paying for his food, his lodging, or buying the tools needed to exploit a life of elegance. (p. 149)

But it was for the former that his family were paying 1,200 francs a year, and for the latter that they gave him a further 1,550 . . .

Rastignac lives on credit, and he gets it, presumably, for the sake of his good looks, elegant appearance, and social connections; and he gets his flat out of Goriot. In 1834, Balzac himself was living on credit and was also in debt. (The irony was that he had worked for it, and earned some quite large sums for his labours (17,000 francs for the eight-volume *Etudes de mœurs au XIXe siècle* in 1833, but only 200 francs per sixteen pages of *Old Goriot* from the *Revue de Paris*, and 3,500 for the first book edition from Werdet). 'J'aurai porté des sacs sur mon dos, j'aurai sué des averses', 'I'll have carried sacks on my back, I'll have sweated blood', Goriot exclaims on p. 207, and so might have Balzac.)

The sheer quantity of financial information given about the characters in *Old Goriot* and the arithmetical and social consistency of most of it (apart from Rastignac's magic money) does not necessarily lend the illusion of reality to the world it depicts; but it gives to the world it creates a particular solidity, a quite specific texture, which it would be unfair to call just an accountant's *tour de force*. Money is treated as a basic constituent of life, as the fundamental element of modern urban life, and in Balzac's insistence on the details of its accumulation and dispersion lies a large part of what he has to say in this novel about French history as it was lived in daily life (see p. 77).

Old Goriot shows us people who earn, spend, lose and worry about money; and it shows us those people living in a world full of things. No novelist before Balzac had seen quite so many things, or thought it proper to mention the material culture of the real world in quite such lengthy detail: but it was in the quality of just such detail, Balzac declared in 1830, that the merit of his works would lie (see p. 9). The long passages of description do not just create an illusion of reality. Indeed, for a modern reader who has never seen nineteenth-century wall-paper or come across Saint Anne marble table-tops, Balzac's descriptions may well create a very imprecise mental picture and a fair amount of confusion. However, these set-pieces (more by their manic insistence on listing everything than by what they actually list), do teach the reader to look, and to see with new eyes. Here are the contents of Madame Vauquer's drawing-room:

Rien n'est plus triste à voir que ce salon meublé de fauteuils et de chaises en étoffe de crin à raies alternativement mates et luisantes. Au milieu se trouve une table ronde à dessus de marbre Sainte-Anne, décorée de ce cabaret en porcelaine blanche ornée de filets d'or, que l'on rencontre partout aujourd'hui. Cette pièce, assez mal planchéiée, est lambrissée à hauteur d'appui. Le surplus des parois est tendu d'un papier verni représentant les principales scènes de *Télémaque*, et dont les classiques personnages sont coloriés. Le panneau d'entre les croisées grillagées offre aux pensionnaires le tableau du festin donné au fils d'Ulysse par Calypso. Depuis quarante ans, cette peinture excite les plaisanteries des jeunes pensionnaires, qui se croient supérieurs à leur position en se moquant du dîner auquel la misère les condamne. La cheminée en pierre, dont le foyer toujours propre atteste qu'il ne s'y fait du feu que dans les grandes occasions, est ornée de deux vases pleines de fleurs artificelles, vieillies et encagées, qui accompagnent une pendule en marbre bleuâtre du plus mauvais goût.   (pp. 28–9)

(Nothing is more sad to see than this drawing-room furnished with armchairs and straight-backed chairs in horse-hair upholstery with alternating dull and shiny stripes. In the middle of the room there is a round table with a Saint Anne marble table-top, adorned with one of those white porcelain plate-holders decorated with gold tracery that has been half rubbed off, of the kind you come across everywhere nowadays. The room, which has pretty poor floorboards, is panelled to shoulder-height. For the rest, the walls are papered with a printed design representing the main scenes of *Télémaque* [a didactic romance published by Fénelon in 1699] with the classical characters coloured in. The panel between the grilled window-frames presents boarders with a picture of Calypso's feast for Ulysses' son. For forty years this painting has aroused the witticisms of young lodgers, who reckon they can rise above their situation by joking about the dinner to which poverty condemns them. The stone fireplace, whose ever-clean hearth is witness to the fact that the fire is made up only for important occasions, is decorated with two vases of artificial flowers that have aged under their wire cages, keeping company with a bluish marble clock in the worst possible taste.)

This is no 'objective' description: it tells you what the room looks like (provided you know what common porcelain plate-holders look like), but it also tells you what to think of its furnishing – the clock is in 'the worst possible taste'. It offers a way of looking at things, in terms of rarity value and in terms of taste; but it also makes you look at things left out of merely entertaining novels, and laugh at them, as the young lodgers do. What else can you do in such miserably impoverished surroundings?

Il s'y rencontre de ces meubles indestructibles, proscrits partout, mais placés là comme le sont les débris de la civilisation aux Incurables. Vous y verriez un baromètre à capucin qui sort quand il pleut, des gravures exécrables qui ôtent l'appétit, toutes encadrées en bois verni à filets dorés; un cartel en écaille incrusté de cuivre; un poêle vert, des quinquets d'Argand où la poussière se combine avec l'huile, une longue table couverte en toile cirée assez grasse pour qu'un facétieux interne y écrive son nom en se servant de son doigt comme de style, des chaises estropiées, de petits paillassons piteux en sparterie qui se déroule toujours sans se perdre jamais, puis des chaufferettes misérables à trous cassés, à charnières défaites, dont le bois se carbonise. Pour expliquer combien ce mobilier est vieux, crevassé, pourri, tremblant, rongé, manchot, borgne, invalide, expirant, il faudrait en faire une description qui retarderait trop l'intérêt de cette histoire, et que les gens pressés ne pardonneraient pas.   (p. 29)

(There you can find some of those indestructible pieces of furniture banished from everywhere else but placed there like the relics of human society are placed at the Hospital for Incurable Diseases. There you'll see a barometer with a hooded monk which comes out to indicate rain, execrable engravings that take away your appetite, all in gold-lined, varnished wooden frames; a hanging wall-clock in a case made of shell inlaid with brass; a green stove, Argand lamps that burn a mixture of oil and dust, a long table covered in an oil-cloth so greasy a cheeky boarder can write his name on it using his finger as a stylus, clapped-out chairs, little cushions made of woven vegetable fibres which are forever unravelling themselves without ever coming to an end, then miserable foot-warmers with broken holes and disconnected hinges, made of wood that's turned into charcoal. To explain just how old, splintered, rotten, shaky, worm-eaten, one-legged, one-eyed, ampu-tated and deceased all this furniture is would require a description which would delay the plot of this history and which people in a hurry would not forgive.)

This joke is on the reader – still at this early stage of the manuscript the elegant lady reader of the *Revue de Paris* (see p. 9) whom Balzac wished to jolt out of her expectation of any easy story (see p. 12). But what is made laughable is not just the technical incompatibility of 'description' and 'history' in the modern sense (in Latin, *historia* means description, as it still does in the term 'natural history', *histoire naturelle*, Cuvier's subject, see p. 72), nor just the pitiful dustbin of Madame Vauquer's establishment, nor just the ultimate vanity of all attempts to portray things with words, but the sheer inex-haustible quantity of material objects produced by early modern industry, with no *raison d'être*, no connection between them, and absolutely no meaning. When Rastignac bursts into a cupboard full of such things in the aristocratic Restaud house, thinking he knows which door to open when he doesn't, the servants laugh:

Rastignac ouvrit la porte . . . mais déboucha fort étourdiment dans une pièce où se trouvait des lampes, des buffets, un appareil à chauffer des serviettes pour le bain . . . Les rires étouffés qu'il entendit dans l'antichambre mirent le comble à sa confusion.   (p. 68)

(Rastignac opened the door . . . but walked distractedly into a room where there were lamps, sideboards, a device for heating bath-towels . . . Smothered laughter from the antechamber embarrassed him thoroughly.)

Humorous descriptions such as these (or Bianchon's parody of Hugo's romantic descriptive style, p. 65) contrast with the usual role of things in the novel. There being no limit to the number of things, nor to the length of a full description of any one of them (compare Balzac's efforts to those of twentieth-century 'New Novelists' such as Alain Robbe-Grillet or of Georges Perec in *Life: A User's Manual*), most objects are included in descriptive passages in novels because they signify something. Goriot's powdered wig ('cheveux en ailes de pigeon', p. 39) signifies his attachment to an older way of life, perhaps to older values, and its disappearance on p. 46 is a clear sign of his impoverishment. The shape of the skull it no longer hides is mentioned (first on p. 67, by Rastignac) because it too means something, at least to Bianchon, whose medical training included the teachings of the science of phrenology. Invented by Franz-Joseph Gall (1758–1828), phrenology (or cranioscopy) studied brain functions and character-traits in terms of the external shape of the skull: Bianchon can see Goriot's one protruding 'bosse', ('bump'), 'celle de la paternité, ('the bump of paternity'), p. 91. Vautrin also wears a wig, to hide his red hair (uncovered on p. 184), which seems to signify energy or wildness ('force mêlée de ruse', p. 184) for Balzac; whilst Victorine's character is as pallid as her complexion ('blancheur maladive', 'sickly pallor', p. 34).

Modern medical science does not recognise any correspondence between the shape of the skull and the particularities of the brain inside it; Gall's doctrines are discredited, and with them Balzac's descriptions of his characters' appearances have become marginally obscure. But this particular instance of a forgotten key to meaning is rather exceptional. By and large the objects and details of appearance which Balzac selects for their meaningfulness in the construction of character and plot are quite as obviously significant to the modern reader as to the original audience, partly because they correspond to very general expectations about human reactions (going pale, blushing, ways of walking and moving) and habitat (the values of darkness and light, cleanliness and dirt, etc. have not changed greatly), and in large measure because Balzac also *explains* what the details signify. Although almost all storytellers set their tales in some kind of setting, and select the details of the setting (however minimal) in terms of their significance to the characters and plot, no novelist before Balzac had invested quite as much of the story in the setting as he did, nor paid such attention to the establishment of atmosphere through a guided interpretation of the inner significance of outwardly apparent detail. The quantitive increase in the details and things seen, and in which significance is seen by the narrator or by characters, produces in *Old Goriot* a qualitative difference in the whole atmosphere of the world represented and the manner of representation. Balzac's descriptive realism is very much a matter of visual density: his world is made to seem chock-full of things, and almost everything in it is chock-full of meaning.

Old Goriot is set in Paris in 1819. It refers a great deal to the physical and geographical realities of the capital, to an extent that makes it seem like a guide to Paris – a tourist guide, mentioning many of the city's monuments and affordable entertainments (watching the elegant parade on the Champs-Elysées, for example, p. 119), a social guide to the principal *quartiers* (see pp. 24–5), and of course a moral guide to life in the city. The novel, which Balzac (in VII) put into the *Scènes de la vie parisienne* section of *The Human Comedy* (transferred to the *Scènes de la vie privée* in VIII), begins by questioning whether it will be understood outside of Paris, and ends, on the last page, with its young hero looking down on the city, 'tortueusement couché le long des deux rives de la Seine', ('curled up along the two banks of the Seine'), p. 254, and fixing his gaze on its central parts, from the column in the place Vendôme (a monument to Napoleon, made from the bronze of cannon captured at Austerlitz) to the dome of Les Invalides (a military hospital and museum). But Paris – 'the central point of the globe where all the lines of magnetic force meet and combine', according to

Balzac's contemporary Jules Michelet – is much more than a setting for the lives of the characters in *Old Goriot*, and more than just a frame for the story. Paris is the only possible setting for the material of Balzac's 'Parisian' novels because it is itself a major part of their material. In a preface to the *Etudes de mœurs au XIXe siècle* probably dictated by Balzac, Félix Davin wrote:

A capital was the only possible setting for these depictions of a period in crisis, where sickness strikes no less at men's hearts than their bodies. Here, true feelings are the exceptions and are broken by the operation of self-interest, crushed by the wheels of this mechanical world; virtue is calumnied, innocence sold, passions yield to ruinous tastes, to vices, everything is evaporated, dissected, bought and sold.   (*Pl*I.1147)

Old Goriot begins well away from the feverish centre of the big city (only London was bigger; Paris had trebled in size, from 650,000 inhabitants to 1,800,000 between the Revolution and the end of Balzac's life) that Davin describes with Balzacian hyperbole (the image of the city as a mechanical wheel is repeated in *Goriot*, p. 27). Balzac takes his reader first to an obscure corner of Paris, where even a Parisian could get lost, which is silent, sombre and depressing – but not at all fictional. The Vauquer boarding-house is located in a real street, rue Neuve-Sainte-Geneviève (now called rue Tournefort) in the back end of the Latin Quarter (then a maze of narrow streets: the big boulevards were not cut through until the 1860s) on the steep southern slope of the Montagne Sainte-Geneviève, beneath the Pantheon and the Sorbonne. It is very probable that it was little used by horse-drawn carriages ('les chevaux la montent et la descendent rarement', 'horses go up or down it very infrequently', p. 27; Anastasie's driver parks higher up, 'au coin de l'Estrapade', 'on the corner of the [place de] l'Estrapade', p. 45) because, prior to the construction of the place Lucien Herr, its gradient must have been very steep (see Castex, xxviii–xxix).

Balzac maintains the same density and accuracy in all his geographical references in *Old Goriot*, and the reader of 1835 could recognise precisely where its characters live and go, if he or she knew Paris, or use the novel as a route-planner through the city's thoroughfares and labyrinths. But since the novel starts in an obscure corner of Paris, almost all readers are thrust into a position where they need a guide, where, like the young law-student come up from the south to learn ('méridional', 'southerner', meant, in Balzac's day, anyone from south of the Loire), they have to trust someone else to show them the way through the labyrinth. 'I give you my name as an Ariadne's thread to go into this labyrinth', Madame de Beauséant says to Rastignac on p. 89. Thus Rastignac, whose assumption of the narrator's role has been discussed above (p. 27), also becomes the reader, in so far as the reader has accepted the role thrust upon him on pp. 25–6 of a student of Paris, and of the passions.

Rastignac finds his way around the streets and buildings of the 'real' Paris pretty easily (but he does make beginner's mistakes: 'To the Beauséant residence!' he tells the cab-driver; 'Which one? asked the driver', p. 75), but the object of his quest is only incidentally the sort of knowledge cab-drivers possess. The inhabitants of this secret (though eventually penetrable) city do impossible things, like entering the boarding-house at night after the door has been bolted. 'You have to stay up all night to really know what's going on around you, in Paris', the narrator tells Eugène on p. 53. But Vautrin stresses how little the student, like the reader, still knows about life in the metropolis:

You're still too young to know Paris well, you'll learn that that's where you find what we call men of passion

In Paris, everything is different, and especially the women:

the comparison he was obliged to draw between his sisters, who had seemed to him so beautiful in his childhood, and the women of Paris . . . multiplied his desire to succeed

The narrator constantly underlines the difference of the women of Paris: 'L'amour à Paris ne ressemble en rien aux autres amours', he tells us on p. 202, 'Love in Paris resembles other loves not at all'. The explicit reminders of the uniqueness of Paris and of the forms of life it fosters complement and support the creation of a Parisian 'atmosphere' through naming real streets, buildings and *quartiers*.

The life that Balzac represents in *Old Goriot* is characterised by the large role played in it by money, by the material objects that surround it, and by the big city in which it is conducted. The detail given in each of these three respects is striking by its quantity and its relatively precise geographical and historical authenticity. But for all its insistence on these constituents of life, *Old Goriot* does not quite turn the tables on the human characters whose stories it tells; Balzac cannot fairly be admired for running ahead of the *nouveau roman* and dissolving his characters into a world subject entirely to the forces of money, things and the city. It's still the people who matter, as they struggle (and, but for Rastignac, fail) to find a balance between the inner propulsions of passion and desire, and outer constraints.

In fact, the Paris of *Old Goriot* is not just an outer setting in which its characters move. The city seems to straddle the distinction between the personal and the impersonal, between 'outer' and 'inner'. At the novel's close, as Rastignac looks down on the city from the hillside cemetery, Paris has become enough like a character for the young man to challenge it, to dream of conquering it, and for a character, Delphine, to seem like a mere figure or symbol for the city. The ways in which Balzac manages to elaborate a mythical and semi-animate city in *Old Goriot* have little to do with descriptive realism as such; but Balzac's particular genius is his ability to write on two levels at once, to give descriptions which are both prosaically accurate, and deeply metaphorical. Paris is the central point of the web of metaphors spun in the text of *Old Goriot*, and it is worth looking at some length at the threads which stretch out from it to all the other parts of the work, producing a very special and perhaps uniquely Balzacian phenomenon, a real city that is utterly mythical, a 'myth of reality' in Barbéris's phrase.

The mythical Paris of *Old Goriot* emerges from the combination of six major images which compare the city, in order to say what it is really like, to an ocean, an underground cavern, a jungle, a battle-field, a mud-pit and finally to a prostitute. (The list is given in order of first occurrence, but since some of the images are repeated more than once, the actual ordering is much more complex, and the mythical object emerges more as a figure woven into a carpet than as a logical sequence of six 'steps' of development.) Each of the images is connected to various pieces of cultural baggage which the French reader may be assumed to have, and it will be difficult to understand the force of Balzac's poetic metaphors without the footnotes appended to the following listing of their major occurrences.

Ocean

p. 34   Mais Paris est un véritable océan (Paris is a veritable ocean)

p. 94   Il avait ainsi quinze mois pour naviguer sur l'océan de Paris (Thus he had fifteen months to sail on the Parisian ocean)

p. 114   ... ceux'ci pêchent des consciences (others fish for consciences)

In 52 BC, the Romans conquered a Celtic village, which they called Lutetia, built on an island in the middle of the Seine, the present-day Ile de la Cité. Since the site was subject to flooding, the Romans built their city on the south (left) bank on the slopes of the Montagne Sainte-Geneviève (see p. 59). After the end of the Roman Empire in the 5th century, the city moved back to the island, and according to legend did so on instructions from its patron Saint Genevieve, despite a flood, to defend itself against Attila the Hun. Seen from above, or drawn on a map, the island is shaped like a boat; and thus, given the frequent flooding, Parisians' constant prayer, which remains the city's motto still today, is that 'the boat should float and not sink' (fluctuat nec mergitur'). Thus the image of Paris as an 'ocean' in *Old Goriot* connects up with the city's legendary origin and its heraldic emblem (the coat of arms of the city depicts a boat) well known to most French readers. This image was, obviously, quite familiar to the novel's first audience; but oceans are also large and fearful things, and the comparison communicates simultaneously the impression of inhuman vastness that Paris can make on its inhabitants, and especially on provincial newcomers, such as Rastignac.

Cavern

p. 26   ainsi que, de marche en marche, le jour diminue et le chant du conducteur se creuse, alors que le voyageur descend aux Catacombes. Comparaison vraie! (just as the light dims and the guide's chant begin to echo as step by step the tourist descends into the Catacombs. A true comparison!)

p. 34   Jetez-y la sonde, vous n'en connaitrez jamais la profondeur . . . il s'y rencontrera toujours un lieu vierge, un antre inconnu (Drop the plumb-line, you'll never know how deep it is . . . there'll always be an undiscovered place, an unknown cavern)

The Romans built their city of Lutetia on the left bank opposite the Ile de la Cité, and beneath it they excavated tunnels for draining the hillside and for use as burial-places. These Catacombs, situated directly beneath the Latin Quarter of nineteenth-century Paris, were one of the more ghoulish sights of the city until the entrances were cemented over in the 1980s. The experience of Paris is thus compared by the narrator to what lay literally beneath Rastignac's first experience of it in the Vauquer lodging-house and law-school.

Jungle

p. 113   Paris, voyez-vous, est comme une forêt du Nouveau-Monde, où s'agitent vingt espèces de peuplades sauvages, les Illinois, les Hurons, qui vivent du produit que donnent les différentes chasses sociales (Paris, you see, is like an American forest bristling with twenty species of wild folk, Illinois, Hurons, living on the produce of different types of social hunting)

A shocking image: in French nineteenth-century opinion, Paris is still the city of light, the 'central point of the globe' in Michelet's words (quoted above, p. 58), and Vautrin's comparison of it to the furthest periphery of the uncivilised world demonstrates how far he takes the 'revolt' he urges on Rastignac as a way of life in French society. But the image reminds the reader of Vautrin's plans to set himself up in the New World – though as a slave-owning planter he would be a long way from Illinois and Hurons.

Battlefield

p. 85   Eugène . . . n'en était qu'à sa première journée sur le champ de bataille de la civilisation parisienne (Eugène . . . had only got as far as his first day on the battlefield of Parisian civilisation)

p. 92   ce subside, avec lequel je dois ouvrir la campagne; car cette vie de Paris est un combat perpétuel (this subsidy with which I must open the campaign; for life in Paris is a constant fight)

p. 254   'A nous deux maintenant!'

The images of battling and battleground (familiar to readers of Stendhal's *Scarlet and Black* (1830)) are all associated with Rastignac, heir to the title of baron and great-nephew of a famous sea-captain. The last words he speaks in the novel are addressed to the city, and, since they are the words used conventionally to initiate a duel, seem to announce a life of combat with the city. But it is not as simple as that, as we shall see below.

Mud-pit

p. 25   cette illustre vallée de plâtras et de ruisseaux noirs de boue (this illustrious vale of plaster . . . and of gutters black with mud)

p. 92   Il s'agit de faire mon chemin ou de rester dans la boue (It's a matter of making my way or staying in the mud)

p. 87   Le monde est un bourbier (Society is a mud-pit)

p. 88   Aussi Madame de Nucingen laperait-elle toute la boue qu'il y a entre la rue Saint-Lazare et la rue de Grenelle pour entrer dans mon salon (That's why Madame de Nucingen would lick up all the mud there is from the rue Saint-Lazare to the rue de Grenelle to have her entry to my salon)

When Balzac was writing *Old Goriot*, Paris had begun to pave its streets with macadam and to install a network of sewers (after the cholera epidemic of 1832), but in 1819 it was still an extremely dirty place with gutters in the middle of the street carrying all rainwater, floodwater, waste and night-soil down to the Seine. Elegance began with a carriage, because without one you could not avoid bespattered shoes and trouserlegs. To stay poor was to stay in the mud, literally; and so mud signifies poverty, in *Old Goriot*, as well as moral turpitude; Rastignac has great difficulty in distinguishing between the two. For some readers, the image of *mud* is the central metaphor of the whole novel, linking the physical with the moral, and giving rise to perhaps the most violently expressive phrase in the book, quoted above from p. 88. But it is not necessarily so, as we shall see.

Prostitute

p. 114   Si les fières aristocraties de toutes les capitales de l'Europe refusent d'admettre dans leurs rangs un millionnaire infâme, Paris lui tend les bras, court à ses fêtes, mange à ses dîners et trinque avec son infamie (The proud aristocracies of all of Europe's capitals may refuse to admit an infamous millionaire to their ranks, but Paris will open him her arms, rush to his parties, eat at his dinners, and share toasts with his infamy)

Symbolic representations of abstract entities (Justice, Faith, Hope, Charity, Liberty) as women have been common from the time of the Greeks, and the standard emblem of France from the Revolution on is the figure of Marianne. There is therefore nothing surprising in the comparison Balzac puts in Vautrin's mouth between the capital city and a woman; and given that Paris had lived with a bewildering succession of regimes and rulers from 1789 to 1834, Balzac's image of the city as a woman of easy virtue is also far from original. In the context of *Old Goriot*, though, the image is made puzzling because it is Paris that makes women truly women for the novel's young hero, Rastignac (see above, pp. 60–1). His desire for Anastasie, then for Delphine (described as a 'passion de commande', 'artificial passion', p. 133) is as much motivated by the ambition to get to grips with Paris as by sexual desire or true emotion for Goriot's daughters. One woman symbolises Paris for Rastignac, Paris is symbolised by a woman for Vautrin: and in the final perspective over Paris, on p. 254, what we see through Rastignac's eyes is a city 'tortueusement couché' ('curled up'), along the two banks of the Seine, words that would also describe a woman, draped on a sofa or divan. Consequently, Rastignac's final challenge, 'A nous deux maintenant' does not only suggest that he is preparing to do battle with the city, or society. Rastignac's combat is also a *combat amoureux*, a battle to be fought principally through the seduction of women, of Parisian women, and thus of the 'woman' that is Paris. Dinner with Delphine is the first realistic step in this career, which will take Rastignac eventually to the House of Lords and the rank of Minister. But the dinner is also a symbol, constructed out of the novel's plot and bringing many of the filaments of the novel's metaphoric web to a final knot, giving a credible but also richly evocative image of a turning point in one young man's life.

There are many more metaphors in *Old Goriot* than those connected with Paris, of course. Vautrin's direct speech is particularly highly charged with metaphor (see below, p. 99), and all of Balzac's characters, from Madame de Beauséant to Madame Vauquer, have frequent recourse to metaphors, comparisons and similes, which serve to characterise the speaker as much as the thing spoken of. In fact, it is not easy to find a novelist other than Proust whose language has anything like the metaphorical density of Balzac's. Stendhal and Flaubert, for example, are much more sparing in their use of figurative language, and tend to say more often what a thing is where Balzac tries to say what it is like. But the Parisian metaphors of *Old Goriot*, because they are colourful, varied and (partly) exotic, without being difficult to understand, serve not so much to explain what Paris was like, as to make it seem strange and different, alternately fearsome (an ocean, a forest) and despicable (a mud-pit, a prostitute). These metaphors bring with them not the reassurance of a set cliché but an emotional charge which transforms the city from an inert place or set of buildings into something more like a character, and for which the term of *myth* seems appropriate. On one level, *Old Goriot* is the tale of a realistic and morally ambivalent young man finding his way between the extremes of love and hatred personified in Goriot and Vautrin in the setting of a city that is, authentically, nineteenth-century Paris; on another level, which co-exists simultaneously with the realistic approach to Paris, it is a telling of the myth of the Great City, in which the stories of Goriot, Vautrin and Rastignac are but particular episodes.

History in the text

Balzac locates the action of *Old Goriot* at a quite precise historical moment, the winter of 1819–20. Secondly, he communicates through the stories he tells a quite broad interpretation of the course of French history in the earlier nineteenth century. The purpose of Balzac's use of historical reference in the novel is similar to his reasons for using as much authentic geographical, financial and material detail as he could, that is to say to beguile his readers into suspending their disbelief and treating imaginary characters as if they were real. But the historical rootedness of *Old Goriot* also serves another purpose, and that is to give a solid foundation to the novel's overall argument about history and its implied warning for the future of French society.

In the early nineteenth century, history and literature were not perceived, as they are now, as radically different enterprises. Michelet's aim, in his monumental *Histoire de France* (1832–47), was to recount the development of the French nation as if it were a novel; and the aims of Sir Walter Scott and Victor Hugo (in *Notre-Dame de Paris*) were to write novels that were properly historical. History, for Balzac, did not belong outside the novel, but was at the very centre of his activity as a writer of fictions. He took the view that as a novelist he could write history that was more properly historical than history

proper; here is how he puts his case in the 1842 introduction to
The Human Comedy:

Reading those dry and rebarbative listings of facts called *histories*, who
has not noticed that writers have forgotten, in all ages, in Egypt, in
Persia, in Greece, in Rome, to give us a history of how life is lived? . . .
French Society was to be the historian, I was to be but the secretary. By
drawing up the inventory of vices and virtues, gathering together the
principal facts of the passions, painting characters, choosing the
principal events of Society, composing types by combining features
drawn from several similar characters, perhaps I would manage to
write that history forgotten by so many historians, the history of how
life is lived. With much patience and much courage, I would complete,
for nineteenth-century France, the book that we all miss, the book
which Rome, Athens, Tyre, Memphis, Persia, India have unfortu-
nately not left us on their civilisations.

(Pl I.10, 11)

Old Goriot does not belong to the literary genre of the historical
novel, as does *Notre-Dame de Paris*, and it contains no real
historical characters. But it does claim to be an 'histoire des
mœurs' (translated above as 'history of how life is lived') and
its stories are made to seem quite remarkably specific to a
particular moment in historical time. Balzac creates that sense
of historical specificity in two principal ways. First, he gives his
characters past lives which engage with major and minor events
in French history. Secondly, he gives some of his characters an
awareness of – but no involvement in – the current events of
1819. It is quite difficult for modern readers to notice this
modest, erudite and surprisingly extensive inscription of history
in the text, because we have become ignorant with the passing
of time. What are scholarly footnotes for us were living
allusions to the readers of the *Revue de Paris*: but one guesses
that even they could learn some of their own recent history from
Old Goriot.

Jean-Joachim Goriot worked for a pasta-maker before the
French Revolution of 1789 (p. 94). His employer fell victim by
chance to the first uprising, which means to say he was
executed, like many others, for no known reason. All the

violence of those turbulent days is brought out in Balzac's almost offhand account of how Goriot was able to buy the business he worked for. He profited from the Revolution and belonged to the new middle class whose interests it served in the longer term. Under the revolutionary government, the sixty 'districts' of Paris were reorganised into 48 'sections', corresponding to the modern *arrondissements* and *quartiers*. Out of calculation ('gros bon sens', 'plain good sense') rather than conviction, Goriot became president of his section, the Halle aux Blés (grain market), and was thus in a position to manipulate prices during the famine of 1792–3 – which, Balzac hints, may have been an artificial famine actually created by profiteers like Goriot. Citizen Goriot grew rich, not out of a straightforward crime of the sort that Vautrin proposes to Rastignac, but out of shady deals in a period when, historically, there was much scope for shady deals. The veracity of this background information has already been underpinned in the novel by the memory of la Duchesse de Langeais, whose mother's estate-manager had sold Goriot quantities of grain at high prices (p. 86). But the Duchesse is an aristocrat, a member of the class which the Revolution had sought to destroy, and she harbours an inherited resentment against the revolutionaries of the Committee of Public Safety, calling them 'coupeurs de têtes', 'head-choppers', assuming that they were corruptly involved in the profiteering of tradesmen like Goriot; and she continues to resent Napoleon, the 'usurper', whose name she mutilates, as did all his aristocratic enemies, to Buonaparte.

These historical references situate Goriot and la Duchesse de Langeais solidly within French history. The doting father does not come from nowhere; he comes from the class of people who were in the right place at the right time to make a fortune out of nothing. But after 1815 when, with the defeat of France at Waterloo, Napoleon's empire came to an end and the Allies reimposed the old Bourbon monarchy in the person of Louis XVIII, Goriot's revolutionary past became a liability. His sons-in-law may reject him for personal, psychological and financial reasons, but their rejection is firmly anchored, in Balzac's account, in the historical reality of the restoration of the monarchy and the accompanying reaction of the right-wing aristocracy against former revolutionaries and the middle classes. 'Vous comprenez bien', 'You won't fail to grasp', says la Duchesse de Langeais to the student Rastignac, and through him to us,

que, sous l'Empire, les deux gendres ne se sont pas trop formalisés d'avoir ce vieux Quatre-vingt-treize chez eux; ça pouvait encore aller avec Buonaparte. Mais quand les Bourbons sont revenus, le bonhomme a gêné monsieur de Restaud, et encore plus le banquier.

(p. 86)

(that under the Empire, the two sons-in-law didn't make any bones about having that old man of 1793 in their homes; under Bonaparte that was still alright. But when the Bourbons came back, the old man was an embarrassment to Restaud, and even more to the banker.)

No significant gaps are left in Goriot's life-story, which is worked out as a historically plausible life engaging with the major political changes which took place in France between the 1780s and 1819. But history also enters *Old Goriot* in the opposite way – as a comic rigmarole perceived by Madame Vauquer, a woman of such little brain that she is wrong in every judgement she makes (about the false comtesse d'Ambermesnil on pp. 41–2, about Goriot's sexual tendencies on pp. 45–7, about Vautrin right up to his arrest, even about her own boarding-house in the comical prospectus given on p. 40). When did she lose her husband? 'Dans les malheurs' ('in the troubles'), p. 30, is all she will say; we may surmise, in the French Revolution (Madame Vauquer, aged about fifty in 1819 (p. 30), would have then been in her twenties), seen not as history but as a nuisance. She sees the massive upheavals of France, from the height of the Revolution in 1792 to the defeat of Napoleon at Waterloo, as a routine backdrop to the main business of life, namely food; her comic lament on the loss of five boarders at once is a parody of broad common sense:

Car, vois-tu, nous avons vu Louis XVI avoir son accident, nous avons vu tomber l'Empereur, nous l'avons vu revenir et retomber, tout cela était dans l'ordre des choses possibles . . . on peut se passer de roi, mais il faut toujours qu'on mange.   (p. 200)

(Because, you know, we've been through Louis XVI having his mishap [decapitated by guillotine on 21 January 1793], the fall of the Emperor [Napoleon I capitulated against overwhelming forces at Fontainebleau on 4 April 1814, exiled to Elba], we've seen his return [landed at Cannes on 1 March 1815 and reassembled French forces for 100 days] and fall a second time [defeated at Waterloo by Wellington and Blücher, 18 June 1815], all that was in the order of things possible . . . You can do without a king, but people can't do without eating)

For once Madame Vauquer is speaking a sort of truth here. France had indeed done without a king from 1793 to 1805 (when it acquired an Emperor), but it had not done without eating except in the dire famine which had made Goriot's fortune. So her lament is both a comic version of history, and a version of Balzac's own claim, quoted above at length (p. 68), that what mattered was not the 'dry and rebarbative listings of facts called *histories*', but the history of life as it is lived – eating and all.

Rastignac has no past life in French history, of course, since he is only nineteen, but he is the heir to a family whose past misfortunes, accounting for the young man's poverty, are typical of a whole social class. Rastignac's father is the nephew of an eighteenth-century naval commander (a colleague of Restaud's grandfather: the world is small!) and the family's fortune, bar the lands it owns south of Angoulême, disappeared overnight when the Revolution nationalised without compensation the enterprise in which the money was invested, the Compagnie des Indes, a colonial trading company modelled on the British East India Company. The entire family history given on p. 72 is fictional, except the existence of the Compagnie des Indes (actually called the *Nouvelle Compagnie des Indes* from 1785) and its suppression, amidst a scandal involving several members of the Convention (revolutionary government) in

1793–4. Many formerly wealthy families of the landed aristocracy were impoverished by revolutionary confiscations: Rastignac, whose parents were lucky enough not to have been forced into emigration or executed at the height of the Terror (1793–4), when the cry in Paris was 'les aristocrates à la lanterne!' ('hang the aristocrats from the lamp-posts!') is in this respect intended to represent a social group which was historically significant in the period after Waterloo, and still alive in the 1830s.

On his restoration to the throne in 1815 (after a short-lived restoration in 1814, interrupted by Napoleon's escape from Elba), Louis XVIII adopted a constitution heavily influenced by the English model, which allowed for a parliament, though with stringent restrictions on the right to vote in parliamentary elections. The first parliament was overwhelmingly reactionary; but in 1818 elections were held which brought into parliament l'abbé Grégoire, a former member of the Convention which had voted Louis XVI's death sentence, and weakened considerably the king's hold on his government. There were disturbances in the streets of Paris – and Balzac's medical student, Horace Bianchon, was there:

I say, the medical student continued, as he came out of Cuvier's lecture at the Zoological Garden, I've just seen that Michonneau woman and that chap Poiret chatting on a bench with a fellow I saw in the disturbances last year near the Chamber of Deputies, and who looked to me like a man from the police dressed up as an ordinary citizen.
(pp. 134–5)

It is almost as if Balzac were trying to give away secrets. Were those 1818 riots the work of police agents, provoking trouble to justify more repressive measures? Bianchon nearly says so, but not quite. But the authenticity of this fictional character is somehow guaranteed, in the conventions now clearly established by Balzac, by his apparently uninvolved presence at an earlier historical event, and his attendance at the celebrated lectures on palaeontology (the first fossils had been discovered at the end of the eighteenth century, and a whole new subject was coming alive) given by Cuvier, attended in reality by many hundreds of young men in 1819, including Honoré de Balzac.

Bianchon is a youthful liberal, and he reads a liberal newspaper, *Le Pilote* (p. 182). Curiously, it is precisely when Balzac's historical memory fails him in some way – *Le Pilote* was not founded until 1821, though it was run, as Balzac says, by Tissot – that he steps in as narrator, explaining how Bianchon could have got news of Taillefer's son's death so quickly. However, the possible view that Bianchon's suspicions of shady dealings in the elections and disturbances of 1818 derive from his political leanings to the left is much more neatly dealt with by a parallel implication in the sermon that Vautrin gives Rastignac, since Vautrin may be suspected of almost anything but liberalism. On p. 109, the criminal holds out to the law student the prospect of becoming a public prosecutor by the age of forty – but only if he performs 'quelques-unes de ces petites bassesses politiques, comme de lire sur un bulletin Villèle au lieu de Manuel' ('one of those squalid little political favours, like reading Villèle [Minister without portfolio in 1820, Finance Minister 1821, Prime Minister 1822] in place of Manuel [elected to parliament in 1818, member of the liberal opposition, expelled from parliament in 1823] on a voting slip').

To the extent that Balzac has anything to say about the details of French political history, he does so indirectly, by allusions that have become imperceptible to all but scholarly eyes. To readers of the *Revue de Paris*, these references to the events of 1818 must already have been somewhat obscure, but we must assume that Balzac intended them to situate his fiction in the half-remembered history of nearly twenty years before. In this sense his work is comparable to that of Cuvier, restoring a living and intelligible shape to the petrified fragments of an age now lost, writing a kind of archaeology of social life which included a memory of political events, but also many humbler reminiscences: songs (like those which Vautrin hums), plays at Paris theatres, books read by characters, all these cultural objects used by characters in *Old Goriot* carry their own date with them, and bring not a vague sense of a grandiose national past, but a feeling of the recent past as it was lived in daily life.

Old Goriot is rooted in a specific historical moment the better to give a sense of the broad trends of historical change in the period following the enormous and unprecedented upheavals of the French Revolution and Napoleon's adventure. Balzac's view, by and large, is that things were getting worse; his huge and detailed panorama of French society in the earlier nineteenth century is unmistakably a story of decline.

It would be wrong to assume that Balzac did not believe at all in progress, to which so many of his contemporaries were passionately attached; but he compares the 'forward movement' of French civilisation to the progression of the chariot of the Indian idol Juggernaut, crushing spectators and worshippers beneath its wheels (p. 26). *Old Goriot*, like many other novels by Balzac, is more concerned with the moral and human consequences of historical change than with any long-term benefits of nineteenth-century 'progress'.

The lives of Rastignac, Delphine and Anastasie are made to seem 'modern' in the novel by Balzac's inclusion of other elements specifically labelled as belonging to the past. He comments as narrator that he cannot put at the centre of a novel of modern life characters like Molière's Alceste or Scott's Jenny Deans (see p. 44), 'magnificent images of probity', because such 'rectangular souls' have disappeared from the modern world (p. 128). But Balzac does sketch in at least one such upright figure on the rural periphery of modern urban life, Rastignac's mother, who reminds the young man of older, better ways in the letter she writes him:

Mon bon Eugène, crois-en le cœur de ta mère, les voies tortueuses ne mènent à rien de grand. La patience et la résignation doivent être les vertus des jeunes gens dans ta position.   (p. 98)

(My dear Eugene, believe it from your mother's heart, devious paths lead to nothing great. Patience and resignation should be the virtues of young people in your position.)

And the warm, innocent fun of the letter from his sister Laure
(pp. 99–101) serves to show Rastignac and the reader that in a
world based on the older values expressed by his mother,
emotions can still be true and pure.

The letters constitute Rastignac's own past – a happy
childhood in the country – and also the past of the novel, a lost
age of innocence. The Goriot family can also look back to a
time of 'paradise', not in the country, but in the commercial
centre of Paris:

Mon paradis était rue de la Jussienne . . . Je crois les voir en ce moment
telles qu'elles étaient . . . Bonjour, papa, disaient-elles . . . Elles me
caressaient gentiment . . . Quand elles étaient rue de la Jussienne, elles
ne raisonnaient pas, elles ne savaient rien du monde, elles m'aimaient
bien.   (p. 236)

(My paradise was in the rue de la Jussienne . . . I can see them now as
they were then . . . Good morning, daddy, they would say . . . They
cuddled me sweetly . . . When they were at the rue de la Jussienne, they
didn't argue, they knew nothing of the world, they liked me.)

The Goriot children, like Rastignac, have grown up into a
world which seems worse than what went before. This is not the
only way of understanding what it means to grow up. By
including his characters' childhoods and presenting them as a
lost paradise, Balzac provides a natural human dimension to
his overall view of history as decline. The field Rastignac enters
with his challenge to Paris on p. 254 does not seem likely to be
the scene of heroic exploits which would change the general
direction of history.

It is easy to see why the mood of 1819–20 might have been
one of pessimism. Four years previously, France had been
humiliated at Waterloo, Paris had been occupied by Russian,
Austrian and English troops for a short period, and the
monarchy, swept away in the Revolution of 1789, had been
restored in the person of Louis XVIII, an obese and impotent
old man; and the constitution through which he ruled had been
virtually dictated by England. But these events are only alluded
to in *Old Goriot* by Madame Vauquer, and they have little

enough to do with the way the novel presupposes and accounts for the sense of historical decline.

In looking back at the period of his own youth with the advantage of fifteen years' hindsight, Balzac could hardly fail to understand it in terms of what had happened between 1819 and 1834. Louis XVIII died in 1824, and was succeeded by his brother who took the title of Charles X. His regime became increasingly autocratic and biased towards the Church; a movement of opposition, coupled with a wave of intellectual ferment in the later 1820s, culminated in a revolt, sparked off by clumsy repressive measures, which was so mishandled by Charles X that in the course of three days (27–9 July 1830) the royal troops were defeated by the people of Paris and the King fled to England. Three young politicians (a lawyer, Adolphe Thiers, and two bankers, Périer and Laffitte) cleverly averted the danger of a Republic being once again proclaimed in France by bringing back to the throne an exiled member of the junior branch of the royal family, Louis-Philippe d'Orléans. The new king was much less regal than his predecessors, styled himself 'roi des Français' not 'roi de France', and lived very much like any wealthy member of the middle classes. He used his power to serve the interests not of the aristocracy, but of the commercial and financial bourgeoisie: his finance minister, Guizot, concluded his first budget speech with the famous exhortation: 'Enrichissez-vous par le travail et par l'épargne!', ('Grow rich through work and savings!').

By the time Balzac wrote *Old Goriot*, it had become very clear that under the July Monarchy of Louis-Philippe there would be no limit set on the social and political power of the moneyed middle classes. That movement of society must have been much less clear in 1819, when the aristocracy had only recently been restored to its positions of power. So when Balzac has Vautrin persuade Rastignac that wealth is the *'ultima ratio mundi'* (p. 89) ('the ultimate root of social life'), or when he has Goriot exclaim that 'monnaie fait tout' (p. 208) ('money does everything'), he is, in a way, *inventing* the past that is needed to make a sense of the present of 1834, a past which contains the origins of the present in a quite explicit way.

Old Goriot offers one very obvious explanation for the decline of human values which it presupposes between the lost paradise of childhood and the modern world (which is in this sense 1834 just as much as 1819), and that is the rule of money. Unlike English novelists of the same period, Balzac is not describing directly or indirectly the effects of the Industrial Revolution: what had begun to happen in the textile mills of the Lille region and in the ironworks at Le Creusot (all much later, and on a smaller scale, than in Manchester or Glasgow) does not impinge on Balzac's Paris, and the working classes have only a marginal existence in *The Human Comedy* – as servants (Christophe, Sylvie and Thérèse in *Old Goriot*) or as the anonymous, distant victims of Nucingen's crookery. What Balzac charts is the rise of commerce and banking, of the middle men, like Goriot and Nucingen, who constitute the middle class of pre-industrial, capitalist society.

Though the rule of money cannot be separated from the rise of the middle classes, the picture Balzac gives of the deleterious effect of the rule of money in *Old Goriot* cannot be construed simply as an attack on the rise of the middle classes. The principal victim of the harsh, money-grabbing society he depicts is none other than the principal representative of the new commercial bourgeoisie, a profiteer and speculator of the first post-revolutionary generation; and one of the main beneficiaries of the novel's action is a hereditary aristocrat (pp. 49–51). This is not done to turn back the clock; but it makes *Old Goriot* a novel written, in a way, against the flow of the historical movement which it demonstrates.

Old Goriot is no doubt historically accurate in showing how far the middle classes still had to go, in 1819, to achieve social dominance. Even if it is money that makes things go round, and even if the Goriots and the Nucingens have plenty of it, what they want to do with it – for their offspring, especially, but also for themselves – is to acquire the prestige of aristocracy, of the aristocracy that had been impoverished, decimated and exiled after 1789 and restored, cautiously, by Napoleon after 1805 (when Nucingen bought the title of Baron), and vindictively by the Bourbon monarchy in 1814 and 1815. The aristocracy, for its part, would like to keep itself quite distinct from the bourgeoisie – it is after all a class defined by breeding, not by occupation or wealth – but few of its members can afford to do so: in *Old Goriot*, only the Beauséants can really choose the company they receive, since only they have kept their great wealth as well as their name. But even the great lady of this noble house (whose name recalls the standard of the Knights Templar, Beaucéant) leaves the scene of Paris, defeated by a poignant instance of the rule of money, her lover's greed for the fortune of the Rochefide heiress.

It is this historical situation alone, a bizarre situation in which two antagonistic social classes, separated by centuries of mutual scorn, by a violent revolution and by a less violent but no less vindictive restoration, come together behind the scenes and in marriage contracts in order to pretend to survive as distinct classes, which allows the plot of *Old Goriot* to make any sense at all; conversely, this plot, in which Rastignac's noble name has a cash value, in which an invitation to Madame de Beauséant's ball is worth as much to Delphine as Restaud's diamonds are worth to Anastasie, must be seen not only as a representation, but as an interpretation of French social history in the Restoration and July Monarchy periods.

What *Old Goriot* argues by demonstration is that the rule of money would destroy the aristocracy from within more surely than the revolutionary expropriations and executions had done. The noble Rastignac will use his inheritance (that is to say, his name) to pursue a special kind of middle-class career: he will succeed as the lover of a trader's daughter married to a banker. The world will be controlled by the Nucingens, the Gobsecks and by adroit manipulators such as Rastignac, not by the Beauséants or the Restauds, except insofar as they connive with the rulers of money. Readers who, whether in the wake of

Marx or of his opponents, see history in terms of economic power, must presumably see *Old Goriot* as giving a generally correct interpretation of history. But Balzac's personal attitude towards the trends he depicts is by no means simple, and to some extent it is simply confused.

As a middle-class writer of the Restoration and July Monarchy period, Balzac was as much in thrall to the prestige of the aristocracy as any of his characters. (He adopted the particle of nobility, 'de', in 1830, after the July Revolution, and later had a coat of arms painted on the door of the tilbury he could not afford.) Madame de Beauséant is more than a representative of a dying class, she is truly a *grande dame* for the novelist, and he requires the reader to admire and pity her:

les personnes les plus élevées ne vivent pas sans chagrins, comme quelques courtisans du peuple voudraient le lui faire croire. (p. 232)

(persons of the highest rank do not live without sadness, as some lickspittles of the populace would like to make it believe)

The grandeur and the suffering of the true aristocrat are values, in the structure of *Old Goriot*, as much as the hard work of the grain-trader, as much as the purity of the Rastignacs' family feelings. The narrator claims at the start that the story he has to tell is a tragedy: 'cette obscure mais effroyable tragédie parisienne' (p. 97) ('this obscure but terrible Parisian tragedy'). Seen as an interpretation of history, Goriot is not a tragedy of the aristocracy in decline, or a tragedy of the bourgeois defeated by his own creation, or a tragedy of the destruction of family bonds: it is a tragedy of all three at once, all three broken by the rule of money. In this way, the novel mobilises the reader's sympathy for values belonging to quite different social classes and historical moments. Like some literary vacuum-cleaner, *Old Goriot* sweeps up aristocratic prestige, commercial speculation, a belief in the family, an admiration for strength even in crime, sentimental attachment to rejected children and even religious sentiment (see p. 82). Partly sincere, partly inherited, partly opportunistic, the novel's amalgam of values, embodied in the character (but not explicitly in the consciousness) of Rastignac is to be seen not so much as the representation, but as the creation of the value-structure or ideology of the modern, moneyed middle class.

The representation of passion

Old Goriot presents itself as a tragedy (p. 97), dealing with passions of such truthfulness that everyone can recognise 'elements' of them in themselves, 'in their hearts, perhaps' (p. 26). In older traditions, grand passions are represented in literature by grand personages – kings or princesses, or mythological figures. Balzac sets himself against such traditions in many ways: by using the novel rather than the stage for his tragedy; by using not sexual love as the material of tragic passion, but paternal sentiment; and by choosing as the vehicle of passion not a grand personage but someone so apparently ordinary as a retired trader. Balzac wishes to argue by example that the passions of ordinary people in ordinary life are just as powerful and just as absolute as the spectacular tragedies of Racine's Phèdre ('the daughter of King Minos and the goddess Pasiphaé') or Shakespeare's Lear. He is therefore obliged to stress two contradictory features of his central figure: on the one hand, Goriot is a perfectly ordinary, everyday fellow, with a comprehensible background and problems that can be explained in a common-sensical way; on the other hand, in order to arouse the appropriate tragic emotions of admiration and pity, Goriot must also be seen to be extraordinary, unique, 'sublime' (p. 131). These two features or dimensions are not really combined, they are superimposed one upon the other. What *Old Goriot* does is to require the reader to believe, or at least to accept, that the everyday world of psychological common sense coexists with a tragic universe of absolute passions.

The common-sense approach to the character of Jean-Joachim Goriot is put to Rastignac by the character called

Muret on pp. 94–7. Goriot's wife died after seven years of marriage. Rather than start a new life with someone else, Goriot chose to transfer all his affective life to the two daughters he was left with. Therefore his 'paternal sentiment' developed to the point of unreason, 'jusqu'à la déraison', filled with all the blocked-off emotion Goriot still felt towards his lost wife. 'Naturally', Muret continues in common-sense vein, he brought up his daughters 'unreasonably'. He spoiled them; by failing to set any boundaries to their demands, he brings them up to expect everything, always, from their father. All this Goriot himself confirms in his extended death-bed monologue on pp. 237–43:

Moi seul ai causé les désordres de mes filles, je les ai gâtées. Elles veulent aujourd'hui les plaisirs comme elles voulaient autrefois du bonbon.   (p. 240)

(I alone am the cause of my daughters' troubles, I spoiled them. Today they want pleasure as they used to want candies)

Muret is clear-sighted enough to see that what Goriot sought in his daughters was not just an outlet for his affection, but also a kind of humiliation, as if he wanted them to punish him – presumably for the death of their mother:

Il mettait ses filles au rang des anges, et nécessairement au-dessus de lui, le pauvre homme! il aimait jusqu'au mal qu'elles lui faisaient
                                                      (p. 97)

(Goriot put his daughters on a par with angels, and necessarily above himself, the poor man! he loved even the pain they caused him)

The self-punishing, self-humiliating aspect of Goriot's relationship with Anastasie and Delphine is similarly confirmed by the old man on his death-bed:

Je les ai habituées à me fouler aux pieds. J'aimais cela, moi!
                                                      (p. 240)

(I accustomed them to treating me like dirt. I liked that, I did!)

The behaviour of Anastasie and Delphine towards their father can therefore be explained by their childhood. They lost their mother, and in an important sense they lost their father too, since Goriot abdicated all authority and control over his daughters. He submitted himself to their childish whims and, since he had ample financial resources, they never discovered any barrier or obstacle in life until they had to deal with marriage and their own sexuality.

The elements picked out so far would make *Old Goriot* a tale of parental inadequacy, a sad but hardly tragic story of the consequences of insufficient parental authority. Unlike Lear, Goriot is not the victim of inexplicable ingratitude, but the victim of his own, almost ordinary, mistakes. But that is not all, and in a sense it is not that at all, that *Old Goriot* has to teach about human emotions.

Goriot defines fatherhood as the abnegation of self in favour of offspring: 'Donner toujours, c'est ce qui fait qu'on est père' ('To give always is what makes one a father'), p. 194. Self-sacrifice is certainly admirable, especially in a culture deeply marked by Christianity. Balzac thought of Goriot as akin to a saint – 'un homme qui est père comme un saint, un martyre, est chrétien' ('a man who is a father in the way that a saint, a martyr, is Christian') *LH* I.257 – and he does not hesitate to suggest such comparisons in the novel. Like the central figure in a Renaissance painting, crowned with a halo or beam of celestial light, Goriot's head, the narrator says, should be the one on which 'all the light of the painting would fall' (p. 38). He could only do justice to 'this Christ of Paternity' if he could use the devices of painters to depict 'the passion suffered for the world by the saviour of men' (p. 197).

What is admirable in Goriot is the exact opposite of what is despicable in Vautrin. The latter is prepared to have murder done in order to collect enough commission to set himself up as a planter with two hundred black slaves in the New World:

Blacks, don't you see? are ready-made children you can do what you like with, without an inquisitive magistrate coming to ask you to account for them.   (p. 212)

Where Vautrin seeks absolute control over substitute children, Goriot offers complete self-sacrifice. Both passions are absolute, and both are in some sense dreams of patriarchy, reflecting each other as mirror-images of the same aspiration to rival not a saint, but God himself.

What *Old Goriot* suggests by juxtaposing Vautrin and Goriot in this way is that passions that seem opposite have much in common: the old lessons that the extremes (of good and bad, love and hate) meet at the edges.

A tragic hero or heroine arouses pity as well as admiration, and is, by definition, trapped in a situation that has no easy resolution. Goriot's trap is of his own making, and is the inevitable consequence of his definition of fatherhood as giving: since what there is to give in the world he inhabits, the world of commerce, namely money, is finite, there must come a point where the giver has no more to give, and ceases, by definition, to be a father. He must move inexorably towards 'the death-throes of paternal sentiment reduced to impotence' (p. 211). Goriot's plight is pitiful. His daughters do not reciprocate the emotion he feels for them in large part because he has accustomed them to treat him as an eternal giver, not as a real person. He has set up such a one-sided relationship that his passion can only express itself through money, and must inevitably run up against the exhaustion of what he has to give. At that point Goriot can no longer be a 'father' in his daughters' view, nor in his own; running out of money destroys fatherhood in the way it has been defined, and necessarily destroys the father.

It is not just a matter of feeling sorry for a man who can only be himself by killing himself, for the victim of a trap. Like the tragic heroines of Racine, Goriot reaches a degree of lucid understanding of himself before he dies. His long self-analysis in the throes of death is a spectacular reversal of the character as he first appears – a dull, mindless old buffer – and contains within it also a carefully prepared but no less spectacular reversal of Goriot's 'paternity'. It is in these two reversals that lies the principal 'truth of the passions' that *Old Goriot* seeks to teach the reader.

All of Goriot's psychological energy is invested in his 'two daughters', ('deux filles'), and as he grows older he has no energy left outside of his passion for more everyday kinds of social interaction. Consequently he appears dull, lifeless, much like Poiret who dines at the same table and who really is 'une espèce de mécanique' ('a kind of clockwork'), p. 33. In a philosophical novel, *Louis Lambert* (1832–3), Balzac argues that all human activity draws on a finite stock of individual energy or 'volonté' or 'fluide vital'. Great men are those able to concentrate their energy on a single object, and in terms of these general notions Vautrin must count as a great man: when he is arrested, he controls his anger by sheer will-power, knowing that for one false move he will be shot:

sa physiognomie présenta un phénomène qui ne peut être comparé qu'à celui de la chaudière pleine de cette vapeur fumeuse qui soulèverait des montagnes, et que dissout en un clin d'œil une goutte d'eau froide   (p. 185)

(his face presented a phenomenon that can only be compared to a boiler full of that steamy vapour which could move mountains, but which a drop of cold water dissolves in an instant)

Goriot is not able to control the 'boiler-valve' of his resources of energy, or money, like Vautrin. Whilst a trader, he is only a trader: 'sorti de sa spécialité . . . il redevenait l'ouvrier grossier et stupide' ('outside of specialism . . . he was no more than the stupid, coarse worker he'd been before'), p. 95. And whilst a father, Goriot is entirely consumed by fatherhood. He does not belong to Balzac's group of 'hommes supérieurs' ('superior men'), p. 115 – which includes, apart from the arch-criminal Vautrin, writers, painters and politicians – but to the class of monomaniacs (Balthazar Claës, see pp. 6–7, old Grandet, in *Eugénie Grandet*, see pp. 7, 16) whose whole indentities are absorbed into a single passion such that it becomes unclear whether they can distinguish their selves from the object of their passions.

Monomaniacs, whether they are train-spotters or alchemists, misers or fathers, are in some sense mad in their refusal to spread their affectivity into the wider domain of social life. Muret certainly thinks of Goriot as a pathological case, and the old man seems to put himself on the lunatic fringe when he declares that, by becoming a father, he understood God:

eh bien! quand j'ai été père, j'ai compris Dieu. Il est tout entier partout, puisque la création est sortie de lui. Monsieur, je suis ainsi avec mes filles   (p. 130)

(Well! when I became a father, I understood God. He is entire everywhere, since creation sprang from him. Sir, that is how I am with my girls)

Monomania verges here into megalomania; and the sentiment of fatherhood seems to become indistinguishable from feelings of maternity.

It takes Vautrin, of course, to see that the mysterious lodger ('too mysterious not to be worth studying', Rastignac says to Bianchon, p. 67) is 'un homme à passions' ('a man of passions'), p. 61. The French reader knows from the title that Goriot is a father ('Old Goriot' is the best available translation of *Le Père Goriot*, as *le père* + surname is a mostly derogatory way of referring to and addressing an old man; but the French title does of course also have the literal sense of 'father', without the priestly connotations that 'Father Goriot' has in English), but Madame Vauquer constructs her own fantastical explanation for her lodger's apparent lifelessness. Offended by Goriot's refusal of her advances when he was still well-off (pp. 39–42), scornful of his growing poverty, Madame Vauquer imagines that the well-dressed women who visit him are not his 'filles' in the sense of daughters, but the other kind of 'filles', namely prostitutes. Thus Goriot becomes an 'old libertine', impoverished by the indulgence of 'strange tastes', and dulled by the medicines used to cure the diseases caught from such activities (p. 49; syphilis was treated with mercury at the time, leaving many patients blind and mad). Madame Vauquer is wrong, of course, but her stupidity serves to establish the theme of

Goriot's sexuality at an early stage in the unfolding of his mystery.

The old man's sexuality emerges in the last happy interlude he enjoys, at the dinner which inaugurates Rastignac's flat in the fashionable rue d'Artois. Here, Goriot hardly behaves like a father:

Il se couchait aux pieds de sa fille pour les baiser; il la regardait longtemps dans les yeux; il frottait sa tête contre sa robe; enfin il faisait des folies comme en aurait fait l'amant le plus jeune et le plus tendre
(p. 198)

(He lay at his daughter's feet, to kiss them; he looked at her straight in the eyes for a long time; he rubbed his head against her dress; in a word, he did the crazy things the youngest and most amorous lover would have done)

It is not surprising that Rastignac feels jealous, and Delphine feels embarrassed: the extreme of 'paternal' love has become indistinguishable from what ought to be, or what needs to be, kept quite separate from it, namely sexual love.

This scene, like Madame Vauquer's projections and fantasies, prepares Goriot and the reader for the content of the dying man's self-analysis on pp. 237–43. Goriot does not reach lucidity easily, and his fatal illness (a barely plausible leakage of cerebral fluid into the skull cavity) causes him intense pain and loss of concentration. But if his mind wanders, it wanders between the two contradictory poles of selfish and unselfish love.

Of course Goriot also hates his daughters. He knows they will not come to him: 'I've known it for ten years. I said it to myself on occasions, but didn't dare believe it' (p. 237). These heartless creatures, guilty of parricide (p. 241), are nonetheless his, and he wants them to belong to him as much as Vautrin wants his slaves:

Je veux mes filles! je les ai faites! elles sont à moi!   (p. 240)

(I want my daughters! I made them! they are mine!)

Goriot also understands that his submission to his daughters
made it impossible for them to love him, made him in his
abjection more a target of hatred than an object of affection.

Elles se sont bien vengées de mon affection, elles m'ont tenaillé comme
des bourreaux   (p. 239)

(They've taken their revenge for my love all right, they've drawn me as
a hangman would)

But if he already knew and felt all this, why did he never seek to
alter a relationship destructive of himself and of his daughters?
He went back to be humiliated 'like a gambler to the game' (p.
239), because all his identity was invested in his 'filles':

Mes filles, c'était mon vice à moi; elles étaient mes maîtresses, enfin
tout!

(My girls, they were *my* vice; they were my mistresses, in short, they
were everything!)

Of course, Goriot means 'mistresses' to be taken metaphorically; he is not confessing to incest here. But he is admitting that
in the greatest sacrifice of the self, there is also great selfishness.
His generosity, of abnegation, to Delphine and Anastasie has
served him and his passion at least as much as it has served
them. And in the extreme of paternal love there is indeed a form
of sexuality, no less powerful for being implied rather than
explicit, which can only be called masochistic, taking pleasure
in pain and humiliation, such that the *filles*/daughters are also
in essence *filles*/prostitutes from whom Goriot has in effect
bought the humiliation he craved ('J'aimais cela, moi!').

   The role given to money in *Old Goriot*, as well as the image of
the city as a woman, and other less striking features such as
Madame Vauquer's misapprehensions of the role of Goriot's
visitors, can now be seen for what they are, the varied elements
of a single, consistent vision of human and social life in complex
interaction. In Goriot's painful self-analysis, Balzac finds the
link between the nature of the social world he has depicted, and

the workings of some of the darker impulses of human nature. In a society where 'l'argent donne tout, même des filles' ('money gets you everything, even girls') (Goriot's words, p. 237), the 'girls', even if they are daughters, are also prostitutes. It is on an insight of this kind that Flaubert was to construct the whole of his *Sentimental Education* (1868); but Balzac shows us the dark side of paternal sentiment as a tragedy, as the lamentable truth behind a passion that remains, in spite of itself, selfless, admirable and virtuous.

Lock claims that the overall 'message' of *Old Goriot* is the trite and unoriginal lamentation that this world is a vale of tears (Lock, p. 59). He sells Balzac short. Goriot's death-bed monologue, delivered in pain and made painful to read, contains a much more interesting lesson about human emotions, a lesson prefiguring some of the claims of modern psychology. Not only does it show how sexuality is somehow involved in all intense passions, even in those that seem most distant from it, such as a father's feelings for his daughters; but also that total passions, such as Goriot's, contain within themselves the whole range of ordinary human emotions – motherly feelings as well as fatherly: 'Or, le sentiment du Père Goriot implique la maternité' ('Thus the feeling of old Goriot implies maternity'), preface to V, *Pl* III.46, hatred as well as love, selfishness as well as self-sacrifice. In the end, Goriot's 'paternal sentiment' is but a figure for human emotion in general, admirable in its affirmation of purity (he loves *only* his daughters), but destructive in its effects in a world that is 'petty, circumscribed and superficial' (p. 234), and utterly contradictory in its sources and its moral value. Balzac was not overselling himself in the opening pages when he claimed that 'everyone' would be able to 'recognise the elements' of the drama of Goriot 'in themselves, in their hearts, perhaps'. *Old Goriot* reminds us particularly powerfully that no strong emotion is unambiguously good or bad; our own feelings are always both.

Modernity

Though he is presented as a worthy object of admiration and
pity, Goriot is no more a model for imitation in life (a 'hero' in
the trivial sense) than are his daughters, or Vautrin. In its final
form, however, *Old Goriot* is the story of Rastignac's education
as well as of Goriot's noble and squalid self-destruction. We
have already seen how the young law student stands in for
Balzac as narrator (see above pp. 16, 27); but he also stands in
for the reader, as the recipient of the teachings offered by the
particular chunks of experience narrated in the novel. For much
of the time, what Rastignac learns is indistinguishable from
what the reader learns; but there are places where the narrator
intervenes to comment on Rastignac's naïvety, ('young pro-
vincials don't know how sweet life can be in a threesome', p. 71)
or his confusion ('to be young, to thirst for social success, to be
hungry for a woman . . .', and the following passage, on p. 53),
when we can learn *from* Rastignac as well as *with* him. He has
two separate literary functions: as an observing eye (the novel's
eye, the reader's), and as an actor in the human comedy, himself
observed   (with   sympathy   and   with   irony)   by   the
novelist/narrator and the reader. Much of the novel's charm, its
ability to enthral, to carry the reader along its rather sinuous
and bumpy paths, derives from our acceptance of Rastignac's
double role, or (as some may prefer to say) from Balzac's skill in
sewing together with almost invisible stitching the two sides of
the fabric of his character.

Almost everything in the novel could be seen as material for
Rastignac's education, which reaches its completion by the end
of the tale: 'his education was coming to an end' we are told
quite firmly on p. 232. Bianchon, for example, not only
provides Rastignac with various elements of knowledge (about
phrenology, medicine, police provocation) but offers his own
good-hearted enthusiasm for study and work as a perfectly
serious model for conducting his life. It is important to realise
that it is not Rastignac but Bianchon, carrying his science

lightly but with firm and simple moral principles (he answers
the parable of the mandarin admirably, confirming Madame de
Rastignac's conviction that 'les voies tortueuses ne mènent à
rien de grand' ('devious paths lead to nothing great'), p. 134,
p. 98) who represents the intellectual 'type' in the microcosm of
the Vauquer boarding house; and that his characterisation
implies very firmly Balzac's belief that the intellect does offer an
escape from the tragedy of passions and the squalor of the rule
of money. Rastignac is tempted by Bianchon's kind of virtue:
he tries to work through the night after his first evening in
society (p. 53), and after Vautrin has tried to teach him a
different lesson, he declares:

Eh bien, non! Je veux travailler noblement, saintement; je veux
travailler jour et nuit, ne devoir ma fortune qu'à ma labeur

(p. 117)

(Well, no! I want to work nobly, with holiness; I want to work day and
night, and owe my fortune to my labours alone)

But Rastignac is incapable of real work: he is neither a scientist
nor an artist, but a student of the law, which is something quite
different; he has an unstable southern temperament (p. 104); his
ordinary needs (for food, p. 31; for sleep: 'il finit . . . par
dormir à poings fermés', 'he ended up . . . sleeping like a log', p.
53) are too great; and he needs to make his fortune quickly, to
allow his sisters to marry well before they're twenty-five
('auront coiffé Sainte-Catherine', as Vautrin puts it, p. 109). His
problems are real enough; but the reader's identification with
him should not be allowed to go so far as to obscure the lesson
taught by Bianchon, not just in *Old Goriot* but in the score of
other novels where he reappears, ever-youthful, ever-cheerful,
and ever devoted to his science – the lesson that hard work and
the search for knowledge provide a virtuous and valuable way
of conducting life even in the 'vale of crumbling plaster and
gutters black with mud' that is nineteenth-century Paris.

Rastignac's double function (as observer, as actor) cor-
responds to the two sides of his moral character: as an observer,
he is wise, generous, and pure, uncontaminated by the evil and

duplicity around him; as an actor he is capable of calculation, selfishness and untruthfulness. We have already seen how Balzac simply superimposes the two levels of Goriot's characterisation – the absolute ordinariness, and the passionate absoluteness – because the coexistence of these two levels is one of the things he wants to make the reader believe in. But the two sides of Rastignac's character are not in principle incompatible, and with his younger hero Balzac creates a complex human being who, like any ordinary person, negotiates his way between the boundaries of good and evil.

With the exception of Victorine Taillefer, 'l'enfant méconnu qui aime son père' ('the unrecognised child who loves her father'), p. 67, the children of *Old Goriot* are an ungrateful and demanding lot. Delphine and Anastasie offer the central examples of filial ingratitude; but the behaviour of Rastignac towards his family allows comparisons to be made which complicate any simple judgement of the girls' behaviour. When he realises how much money he needs just to get a toe-hold in the upper ranks of Parisian society to which he belongs by the thinnest of genealogical threads, he writes the following letter to his mother in the country:

'Ma chère mère, vois si tu n'as pas une troisième mamelle à t'ouvrir pour moi. Je suis dans une situation à faire promptement fortune. J'ai besoin de douze cents francs, et il me les faut à tout prix. Ne dis rien de ma demande à mon père, il s'y opposerait peut-être, et si je n'avais pas cet argent je serais en proie à un désespoir qui me conduirait à me brûler la cervelle. Je t'expliquerai mes motifs aussitôt que je te verrai, car il faudrait t'écrire des volumes pour te faire comprendre la situation dans laquelle je suis. Je n'ai pas joué, ma bonne mère, je ne dois rien; mais si tu tiens à me conserver la vie que tu m'as donnée, il faut me trouver cette somme. Enfin, je vais chez la vicomtesse de Beauséant, qui m'a pris sous sa protection. Je dois aller dans le monde, et n'ai pas un sou pour avoir des gants propres. Je saurai ne manger que du pain, ne boire que de l'eau, je jeûnerai au besoin; mais je ne puis me passer des outils avec lesquels on pioche la vigne dans ce pays-ci! Il s'agit pour moi de faire mon chemin ou de rester dans la boue. Je sais toutes les espérances que vous avez mises en moi, et veux les réaliser promptement. Ma bonne mère, vends quelques-uns de tes anciens bijoux . . .'   (p. 92)

('My dear mother, see if you haven't got a third nipple to open for me. I am in a position to make my fortune quickly. I need twelve hundred francs, and I need them at all costs. Don't say anything about my request to my father, he might set himself against it, and if I were not to have the money I would be in such a despair as to blow my brains out. I'll explain my reason as soon as I see you, because I would have to write volumes to make you understand the situation I am in. I haven't gambled, my dear mother, I don't have any debts; but if you want to preserve the life you gave me, you have to find me that sum. In brief, I am received by the vicomtesse de Beauséant, who has taken me under her wing. I have to move in society, but I haven't got a penny to get clean gloves. I'll manage if I only eat bread, and only drink water, I'll fast if I have to; but I cannot do without the tools you spade the vine with in this part of the world! It's a matter of my making my way in the world, or staying in the gutter. I know all the hopes you have placed in me, and I want to fulfil them quickly. Dear mother, sell some of your old jewels . . .)

Rastignac's demand is brutally direct and the metaphor he uses is as strikingly forceful as any of Vautrin's (see p. 99); he appeals straightforwardly to his mother's physical role as mother and asks her to find a third nipple from which he may suck not milk but money. But alongside the demanding baby, Rastignac is also the growing child who recognises that the Father may say no. To ensure that his mother treats him as a baby whose demands have to be met, and not as a child subject to paternal authority, Rastignac cruelly blackmails her with the threat of suicide. The letter then moves into a rather chaotic list of protestations of innocence ('I've not gambled . . . I'm not in debt'), partial explanations ('I have to move in high society'), declarations of rather puerile courage ('I'll manage on bread and water . . .') and self-justifications ('I know how many hopes you have placed in me, and I want to fulfil them rapidly') before making the real demand: sell your jewels and, if necessary, your sister's old lace.

But Balzac's selfish careerist also has a moral conscience near the surface: 'Il avait honte d'avoir écrit' (p. 93), and, in conflict with himself, he hesitates until the last moment before posting the letter. He comforts his shame by turning his extortion of family resources into an act of bravado: '"Je réussirai!" Le mot du joueur, du grand capitaine . . .' ('"I'll succeed!" The gambler's phrase, the word of a great leader . . .'), p. 93 – but it is clear to Rastignac that there is not necessarily any greater bravery in his appeal for funds than in Delphine's and Anastasie's repeated demands on their father's purse. On reading his mother's reply, he accuses himself of being a worthless son:

Ta mère a tordu ses bijoux! se disait-il. Ta tante a pleuré sans doute en vendant quelques-unes de ses reliques! De quel droit maudirais-tu Anastasie? Tu viens d'imiter pour l'égoïsme de ton avenir ce qu'elle a fait pour son amant! Qui, d'elle ou de toi, vaut mieux?   (p. 99)

(Your mother has melted down her jewels! he thought. Your aunt must have cried on selling some of her ancient possessions! By what right can you condemn Anastasie? For the sake of your own selfish future you have just copied what she did for her lover! Which of you is worth the more?)

Of course the reader tends to give Rastignac 'more worth' precisely because he is able to doubt himself, and to ask questions about his own moral value. Rastignac's duality can be accounted for as the result of his double function as observer and as actor (see p. 90), and (in instances such as these) as an observer of himself as actor; but what grows out of the problem or opportunity created by his double function in the shifting structure of *Old Goriot* is what most readers have now come to expect in a novelistic character, a reflexive consciousness, a 'rounded' character holding together contradictory aspects of what emerges as a single psychology. For this reason, Balzac never makes his final attitude to Rastignac clear. The creator of this complex, modern character always hedges between two views of his nature, not just in *Old Goriot* but also in all of the 'later' texts (some written, of course, prior to *Goriot*) where the successful *parvenu* reappears as lover, as swindler, as statesman, and finally as a minister married to the daughter of Delphine – possibly his own daughter: Balzac never quite resolves the contradiction between Rastignac's emotional sensitivity, and his ruthless, selfish pursuit of wealth and status, because the whole point of Rastignac is to be morally indeterminate, to be in a constant state of uncertain negotiation between good and evil, to be situated in real life, in the fuzzy borderline area between what is right, and what you can get away with.

Unlike Stendhal's Julien Sorel, in *Scarlet and Black* (1830), who also seeks status and wealth from an unpromising start in life and achieves a great deal through women, Rastignac neither falls in love, nor dies at any point in *The Human Comedy*. That is the simplest way of pointing out how Rastignac is neither a romantic hero nor a tragic figure, but a model of real life. What is more, love and sex play secondary roles in his 'education' in *Old Goriot*. Although it is never stated outright (the *Revue de Paris* would not have taken such explicitness in any case: see p. 8), it is hinted fairly clearly that Rastignac is a virgin at the outset of the novel. 'Moi et la vie, nous sommes comme un jeune homme et sa fiancée ('Me and life, we're like a young man and his bride-to-be'), p. 117, the student declares to himself, using an image which suggests very strongly even if it does not actually state that Rastignac has yet to get into bed metaphorically with 'life' (which only women understand properly, he says to Madame de Beauséant, p. 81) or literally with a woman. A few pages later, the narrator compares Rastignac not to a virginal young man, but to a young girl, with an allusion to the abused virgin of Rojas's *Celestina*:

La parole de Vautrin . . . s'était logée dans son cœur comme dans le souvenir d'une vierge se grave le profil ignoble d'une vieille marchande à la toilette, qui a dit 'Or et amour à flots' (p. 120)

(Vautrin's words . . . had lodged in his heart just as the ugly profile of the old clothes-seller, promising 'Money and love without end', imprints itself in the memory of a virgin)

The manuscript also gives another strong hint to what Balzac no doubt intended us to understand about Rastignac's youthfulness and purity. In the passage on p. 73 where Anastasie tells her lover Maxime de Trailles not to be jealous of Rastignac because he will be useful as a 'lightning-conductor' for

Restaud's jealousy, she refers to him in the manuscript as a 'petit lycéen' ('little schoolboy') (Barbéris, p. 229), corrected to 'petit étudiant' in **III**. The 'schoolboy' loses his virginity in the course of his education, to be sure, but it is both a long-delayed and a curiously peripheral element in that education. Delphine has certainly not slept with him before p. 150, since the narrator states that 'elle hésitait à lui donner réellement les droits dont il paraissait jouïr' ('she held back from according him in reality the rights he appeared to enjoy'). She delays her favours until she has what she wants from her aristocratic connection: 'Devinez ce que je vous apporte' ('Guess what I've brought you') Eugène says on p. 203, referring to the invitation to the Beauséant ball; and on p. 204, Delphine declares 'aujourd'hui je veux être tout heureuse', ('today I want to be completely happy'), and keeps Eugène until one in the morning . . .

The prudery of the nineteenth century obliges Balzac to proceed in this indirect way to say what needs to be said about the difference of his young hero from other heroes of novels and romances. Rastignac's virginity, as a metaphor for his disengagement from the passionate entanglements of Goriot, Anastasie, Vautrin and so forth, and as a literal state of affairs, is more important in this novel than the young man's loss of virginity, which occurs as a reward for a social service, and not as the fruit of passion. The ordinary obsession of a nineteen-year-old, and the ordinary hidden centre of romances of all ages, is displaced from the centre of Rastignac's education: neither sex nor true love provide him with his path to maturity. As he brings his pursuit of Delphine to consummation, the plight of the father weighs upon his heart; and he sheds 'the last tear of his youth', p. 253, not for a woman, but for the death of a father.

Rastignac's disengagement from the usual emotional accompaniment to sexual initiation makes it seem as though he has learnt with ease and alacrity the lesson that Madame de Beauséant teaches on pp. 80–9. This drawing-room sermon is delivered by a woman cruelly betrayed by her supposed friend, la duchesse de Langeais, and on the point of being deserted by her lover, Ajuda-Pinto. It is against the latter that her bitterness is directed, as her involuntary and uncorrected mistake of addressing Rastignac as 'Miguel' (p. 88) reveals. (This slip shows Balzac at his most perceptive; on the other hand, Madame de Beauséant's extremely vulgar 'Hein?' on p. 80 was reckoned by nineteenth-century critics to be a Balzacian howler, since a lady of such noble rank could not possibly have uttered such a grunt – or so they claimed.) Madame de Beauséant feels, not without justification, that she has been used as a stepping-stone to a wealthy bride of an age to bear Ajuda-Pinto's children and legal heirs; and so she generalises, claiming that all Parisian careers are based on the heartless manipulation of women, and urges Rastignac, if he wishes to succeed (she uses the term 'réussir'; Vautrin, and Rastignac, use the more special, modern term, 'parvenir'), to treat women like horses, and to leave them behind at each staging-post in his career. He must therefore hide his real feelings, if he has any, to avoid being taken for a ride himself:

Vous pourrez alors tout vouloir, vous aurez le pied partout. Vous saurez alors ce qu'est le monde, une réunion de dupes et de fripons
(p. 88)

(Then you will be able to wish for everything, you will hold your own everywhere. You'll know what the world really is, a collection of fools and scoundrels)

It's not clear whether this paranoid view of humanity, composed uniquely of two classes, fools–victims–losers and scoundrels–operators–winners, refers to 'the world' as a whole, or only to that part of the world, high society (a regular meaning of 'le monde' in Balzac's French), which Madame de Beauséant knows. In either sense, Madame de Beauséant contradicts herself implicitly by telling Rastignac to be neither a fool nor a scoundrel: it is not clear what else he could be if he accepts his mentor's division of humanity, or society. The young observer, with his 'esprit sagace', 'wise mind', p. 31, is not fooled, since later that evening he recalls these words as 'the lessons torn from Madame de Beauséant by the anger of a deserted woman', p. 90. Trapped by her anger, and isolated by her perception of all around her as either 'operators' or 'victims', she is propelled by her own emotional logic to self-destruction, at least in terms of her social life, and after her ball withdraws to lead a life of rural solitude at Courcelles in Normandy. Rastignac, however, is not inclined to reach that kind of conclusion, nor even to take his second cousin's sermon at face value. How could he? He is young and hungry (p. 31) and he is overwhelmed by the grace and luxury of the aristocratic interior he has just visited for the first time in his life. In the event, Madame de Beauséant's description of human relations is not obviously contradicted by anything that happens in high society in the rest of the novel; and her lesson of emotional disengagement (but not her example of withdrawal) is one Rastignac seems to know how to use already. Adult life in that society, 'infâme et méchant' ('infamous and evil') as it may be, is a far too alluring prospect to be abandoned for the sake of emotional transparency.

The drawing-room sermon thus contributes directly to Rastignac's education, and lodges in his memory; but it also serves to fulfil a reader-related function. Madame de Beauséant offers a very simple moral interpretation of the novel's subsequent action. Her words motivate and justify in advance a simple reading of Rastignac's adventures (as actor not observer) as a descent into immorality, into the *bourbier*, the moral mud-pit of Parisian society. Of course Balzac means this reading to be a perfectly valid way of understanding what happens; but he also offers the reader other ways of understanding life.

The second and longer sermon preached to Rastignac by Vautrin (on pp. 106–16) is, despite its wealth of picturesque detail, as simple and simplistic as Madame de Beauséant's. Coming from the other end of the social spectrum, Vautrin's lesson also divides society into two classes of 'operators' and 'victims'. The difference is that for Vautrin the operators are few in number and are superior, rather than inferior men, outright criminals rather than merely selfish lovers; whilst the victims of 'votre désordre social' ('your social disorder'), p. 107, comprise more or less everybody, from workers to magistrates, who muddle on in mediocrity and the hypocrisy born of compromise. In that Vautrin also divides the world into two classes, Rastignac is correct to claim (p. 116) that his lesson is a vulgar version of Madame de Beauséant's. Like the great lady, the criminal also urges Rastignac to use other people in order to achieve status and wealth; and his offer of a bizarre murder plot parallels Madame de Beauséant's offer to introduce Rastignac to Delphine de Nucingen and to invite her to the great ball.

These similarities are of course not fortuitous and constitute one of the more obvious internal repetitions, or elements of structure, in the novel. Both instances of paranoia are also given similar psychological motivation: Vautrin, like Madame de Beauséant, has suffered an experience of emotional loss and betrayal, but a long time earlier, in his youth:

I was a child, I was your age, twenty-one. I still believed in something, in the love of a woman, a lot of nonsense . . .   (p. 107)

Vautrin seems to have retreated from this hurt into a hidden society that is comprised exclusively of men, which follows its own internal code of honour, and conducts a permanent war with 'official' society. But it cannot be insignificant that despite the *Society of the Ten Thousand*, despite the wealth he has at his disposal, and despite all his physical, verbal and intellectual strength, Vautrin is trapped by the two least intelligent and least human boarders at the Vauquer lodging-house, Michonneau and Poiret. Like Madame de Beauséant, he is forced off the stage of Rastignac's education. His lesson, like hers, is dispensable once it has been truly learnt. What Rastignac learns from him and from Madame de Beauséant, it seems to me, and of course from Goriot's more difficult example, is that absolute answers – be they of good or of evil – do not take him where he wants to go, and will not earn dowries for his sisters.

Vautrin's colourful speech, like Madame de Beauséant's, can also allow the reader to make a simple and limited interpretation, to close off some of the more difficult readings. It offers a whole set of possible answers to the problem of becoming an adult in a morally mixed and complex society. If s/he wishes, the reader can accept Vautrin's resentment of social life – 'il faut vous manger les uns les autres comme des araignées dans un pot' ('you have to eat each other up like spiders trapped in a jar'), p. 110 – and retreat with him into megalomania: 'Il faut entrer dans cette masse d'hommes comme un boulet de canon' ('You have to burst into the mass of men like a cannon-ball'), p. 110, and into cynicism: 'ça n'est pas plus beau que la cuisine, et ça pue tout autant' ('it's no more nice to look at than a kitchen, and it stinks just the same'), p. 111. 'La Révolte' as a way of life may indeed seem attractive, particularly when supported by a monosexual, and possibly sexless, Boy Scout fraternity; and readers who feel so attracted might well see Rastignac's hesitant and ambiguous response to Vautrin's forceful preaching of the perfect crime as spineless wavering. But if we wish to learn from the novel what it is that Rastignac learns, it would be better to resist as he does Vautrin's attempt to impose a logically consistent and passionately simple answer to the real problem of how to survive and succeed in the modern world.

If it were possible to summarise adequately exactly what it is that Rastignac learns in order to survive, *Old Goriot* would not be a novel but a treatise. Despite this reservation, we can attempt to circumscribe what it is that Balzac wanted his reader to understand through the mode of his fiction about the qualities engendered in an intelligent, sensitive young man in some respects like himself, and in other respects (particularly appearance) like the younger Adolphe Thiers (who long after Balzac's death would indeed become a conservative Prime Minister of the nascent Third Republic) by the nature of the society he invented to represent the origins of the real society he and his readers were living in.

Ambition is not presented as evil in itself in *Old Goriot*; but

Rastignac's experiences are there to show how evil is present in all aspects of a society ruled by money. Passion is not unworthy of admiration and pity, but Rastignac sees how its effects are destructive, and learns to control his own emotional life: he keeps it within the family, his surrogate Parisian family, in which he is the only true connecter between the generations, loving the father and having a love-affair with the ungrateful daughter, and in the end marrying the granddaughter. Survival must involve compromise with evil and control of the passionate side of one's own human nature: so it seems that what Rastignac learns is implicit already in his original function as the observing eye of the narrative: the 'operators' who survive and thrive are those who never become victims because they remain, fundamentally, observers of tragedy and of the human comedy, and never engage their own selves totally in an enterprise (alchemy, paternity, love) lying totally outside of themselves. As an actor, Rastignac conducts his life in the closed circuit of a single adoptive family. Of all that lies outside, he is an observer bent on understanding: and it is understanding, rather than involvement, which is the key offered by the example of Rastignac.

All three of the central characters of the novel can be seen, finally, as partial representatives of the novelist himself, and they no doubt owe some of their ability to come alive as real characters in the reading of the text to the way in which Balzac has invested himself in them. Vautrin is at war with 'society': his powerful denunciation of hypocrisy, and his secret means of control, are analogous to the narrator's initial denunciation of his readers' hypocritical tastes, and to his art of narrative control. Goriot consumes himself in his attempt to continue being father and mother to his daughters: his gift of life, and of the stuff of social life, can be seen as an image of the novelist's unending struggle to give birth to 'living' characters. Rastignac, like the novelist and historian, is an observer and student of life. Balzac's realism, consciously angled towards the authentic representation of things and people 'out there', does not prevent his novel from being at the same time, and on a different level, an imaginary and multiple representation of the writer himself.

Bibliography

Translations

The most recent English translation of *Old Goriot*, by Marion Ayton Crawford, is now over 30 years old, but remains available in paperback edition published by Penguin.

Works directly referred to

Auerbach, Erich. *Mimesis. The Representation of Reality in Western Literature* (1946). Princeton U.P., 1953.

Balzac, Honoré de, *Le Père Goriot*, ed. P.-G. Castex. Paris, Classiques Garnier, 1963.

Barbéris, Pierre. *Balzac. Une Mythologie réaliste*. Paris, Larousse, 1971.

'Le Père Goriot' de Balzac. Ecriture, structures, signification. Paris, Larousse, 1972.

Chollet, Roland. *Balzac journaliste. Le Tournant de 1830*. Paris, Klincksieck, 1983.

Flaubert, Gustave. *Correspondance*, ed. J. Bruneau. Paris, Gallimard (Bibliothèque de la Pleïade), 1976.

Hugo, Victor. *Notre-Dame de Paris*, ed. J. Seebacher. Paris, Gallimard (Bibliothèque de la Pleïade), 1975.

Levin, Harry. *The Gates of Horn* (1963). New York, Oxford University Press, 1966.

Lock, Peter. *Balzac: 'Le Père Goriot'*. London, Edward Arnold (Studies in French Literature, 11), 1967.

Maurois, André. *Prométhée ou la vie de Balzac*. Paris, Hachette, 1965.

Ronai, Paul. 'Tuer le Mandarin', *Revue de littérature comparée*, July–September 1930.

Uffenbeck, Lorin. 'Balzac a-t-il connu Goriot?', *L'Année balzacienne*, 1970, pp. 175–82.

Other studies of *Le Père Goriot*

Fortassier, Rose. Introduction to *Le Père Goriot*, Pl III.3–36.

Gaudon, Jean. 'Sur la chronologie du *Père Goriot*', *L'Année balzacienne*, 1967, pp. 147–56.

Hoffmann, Léon-François. 'Les Métaphores animales dans *Le Père Goriot*', *L'Année balzacienne*, 1963, pp. 91–106.

Mozet, Nicole. 'La Description de la Maison Vauquer', *L'Année balzacienne*, 1972, pp. 97–130.

Approaches to Balzac

Bardèche, Maurice. *Une Lecture de Balzac*. Paris, Les Sept Couleurs, 1964.

Barthes, Roland. *S/Z*. Paris, Le Seuil, 1970. English translation, New York, Hill & Wang, 1974.

Curtius, Ernst-Robert. *Balzac*. Paris, Grasset, 1936.

Hunt, Herbert. *Balzac's 'Comédie humaine'*. London, The Athlone Press, 1959.

Lukács, Georg. *Studies in European Realism* (1950). London, Merlin Press, 1972.

Picon, Gaëtan. *Balzac par lui-même*. Paris, Le Seuil, 1957.